# GRANNY SQUARE ACADEMY 2

*by Shelley Husband*

Cracking the granny square crochet code

**ISBN:** 978-0-6485640-8-9

**Charts made by Amy Gunderson**

Email: kinglouiespizza@gmail.com

Ravelry ID: AmyGunderson

**Graphic Design by Michelle Lorimer**

Email: hello@michellelorimer.com

**Technical Editing by SiewBee Pond**

Email: essbee1995@yahoo.com

**Photography by Shelley Husband**

First edition 2023

Published by Shelley Husband

PO Box 11

Narrawong VIC 3285

Australia

**shelleyhusbandcrochet.com**

0824

# Contents

# Contents

# Welcome to Granny Square Academy 2!

Thanks so much for choosing to extend your crochet knowledge and improve your skills with the second instalment of Granny Square Academy.

While it is not necessary to have completed the original Granny Square Academy, it is recommended if you are new to granny squares. A lot of the things covered in this book assume you have some knowledge of crochet and granny squares, as well as the stitches and techniques covered in the first book.

# Navigating Granny Square Academy 2

I have written this companion to Granny Square Academy to be worked from front to back. Each part teaches you something new, building on the previous parts.

## The Parts

In each part you will find:

### Topic Reading

I explain the topics for the part and the new stitches or techniques in detail. Why you do it. How you do it. That kind of thing. As well as tips and tricks to make your crochet sing.

### Patterns

Each part has a written pattern in both UK and US terms, and the charted form for you to practise each lesson. Left-handed versions of the charts can be found in the digital version.

### Pattern Help

At the start of each Pattern Help section, there's a list of prior knowledge needed from the first Granny Square Academy.

This is followed by help for the parts of the pattern that may be new to you or trip you up, with detailed explanations and photos.

### Round by Round Photos

A photo of every round of the pattern for quick checking against as you work.

## After the Parts

After the twelve parts, you will find more handy tips and information.

### Border pattern

A simple border you can use to frame blankets.

### Project Planner

Use this to record your progress. Record your yarn and hook information, square sizes, how many you make, and how much yarn each one uses so you can plan your own project using the twelve patterns.

### Glossary

A written description and chart symbol for all stitches and techniques used in the twelve patterns.

### Pattern list

This list shows the stitch count of each pattern and the amount of yarn needed to make one square in 8 ply/DK/light worsted yarn.

 *Scan QR code to download the digital version of this book.*

## Pattern size

Just like in the first Granny Square Academy, all squares should work out to be the same size if you use the same yarn and hook to make them. Plus, these patterns will match in size to the first GSA patterns.

If you find a small variation in size, either block to size or, if that's not possible, add a round of small stitches to make up the difference. You will find joining also evens out small differences in size. I talk more about size differences and the reasons for them throughout the book.

For me, using 8 ply/DK/light worsted cotton and a 4.5 mm hook, the squares measure 5.5 inches across. The size of your squares will depend on your yarn and hook combination and your crochet style. You don't have to get the same result as me! A square is a square, no matter the size.

## You will need

- Yarn
- Hook
- Scissors
- Yarn needle
- Crochet stitch markers
- Tape measure
- Blocking board and pins

You can use any yarn and hook to work through the lessons.

I used 170 grams/415 metres to make one of each of the twelve patterns of 8 ply/DK/light worsted cotton.

The intention of this book is to teach you stitches and techniques. There are no specific projects to make, but you will find some help explaining how to plan a project in Part 12, as well as the details of the sampler blanket I made. There is also a Project Planner worksheet you can use on page 190.

### TIP

**While learning, I recommend a solid, single colour yarn to make reading your crochet easier.**

Start with the hook size recommended for your yarn. If you find the fabric of your granny squares is too dense or loose for your liking, experiment with other hook sizes.

Let's get started!

# Part One

## Reading

## Patterns

## Look Behind Vivien Pattern Help

## How to start a granny square

Let's kick off by exploring a few ways you can start a granny square.

### The traditional way

A common way to begin granny squares is how you may have learned originally, crocheting a length of chain and slip stitching into the first chain to create a ring to work into.

This can leave a large, bulky hole in the centre of your granny square.

## A neater option

Then, there is how most patterns began in the first Granny Square Academy, attaching your yarn to your hook with a slip knot, chaining 1 and working all the Round 1 stitches into that single chain.

How you make your slip knot matters. As does how you work into the first chain. Depending how you do those two things, you may find your chain 1 opening up into a big loose ring. Or, you may find your first chain disappears as you make other chains, making it hard to see and work into.

You can fix the loop opening by cinching it closed as you weave in the end.

To avoid the first chain disappearing or being too tight to work into, you need to be mindful of how you make your slip knot.

Make your slip knot by pulling the yarn through the loop from your ball of yarn i.e. the working yarn, not the tail.

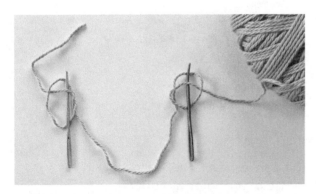

*Silver needle – drawing through tail. Red needle – drawing through working yarn from ball.*

Then, work your Round 1 stitches over the top 2 strands of the chain 1.

> **NOTE**
>
> **This method works best for patterns with up to 12 stitches in the first round, as it's tricky to get more than 12 stitches into a single chain.**

## Magic circle

All patterns in this book recommend starting with a magic circle. This is the way I begin the vast majority of my granny squares. If I don't, it's usually because I want a different effect in the centre and will describe another way to begin as shown in this photo. It is the start of my Flores pattern from Siren's Atlas.

## How to make a Magic Circle

A magic circle is really just a slip knot (as shown on the previous page) not pulled tight, with a chain to anchor it.

I do this in all the pattern videos. Here's how to do it.

Begin as you would a slip knot, make a loop and pull the working yarn through the loop.

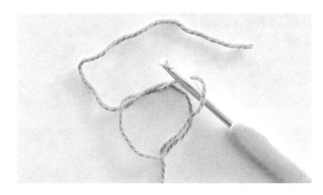

Twist your hook upwards and make one chain.

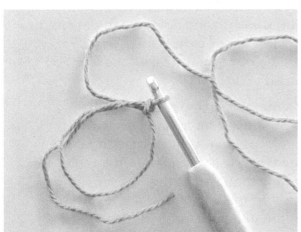

That's it! Now work your Round 1 stitches over the 2 strands of yarn to the left. This will be flipped for left-handers and you will work over the 2 strands to the right.

Pull the magic circle closed once you have made all Round 1 stitches. Hold the base of the last stitch made as you pull the tail tightly, and the centre hole will disappear – like magic!

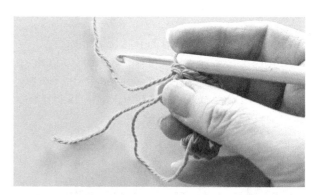

## NOTE

Use caution with fine, delicate yarns. They can break when pulling the magic circle closed if pulled too hard.

### Tips for using a magic circle

The thing to note about using a magic circle is that there is no knot, so if you are not diligent about weaving in your end, it can come undone with washing and use. But don't let that scare you.

## TIP

**Be generous with your magic circle tail. This is not a time to save an inch or two. You need a good length of tail to weave the end in well.**

All you need to remember is to change directions two or three times when weaving in your end, making sure you anchor each change of direction by going over the strand of yarn you last came out of.

You are not limited to weaving into the base of the first round of stiches. You can also weave in your end into other rounds, remembering to anchor each time you change direction.

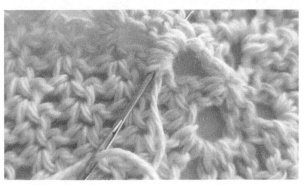

Your yarn fibre and construction will impact how likely your end is to work its way loose. A shiny, machined, smooth yarn will be much more likely to wriggle loose than a natural wool with its spiky fibres. The smoother it is, the more diligent you need to be with your end weaving.

You can make a double ring to work into if you wish. I tend not to do this as I find it trickier to pull closed and it only saves you a little bit of weaving in of the end. You still need to do it well.

Remember, in most patterns, the instructions describing how to begin are usually a recommendation. You can generally use your preferred method. Be aware though that the way you decide to start may affect the look of your granny squares.

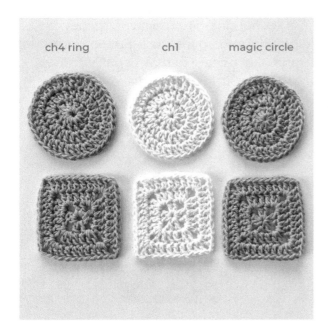

ch4 ring | ch1 | magic circle

The differences are small in these patterns and all starting methods work, but small things can have a big impact on the overall result. There are some patterns where how you begin is really important.

# Alternative to chain at the start of rounds

I like my crochet to look as seamless as possible, so while I state in my patterns the traditional length of chain at the start of rounds to take the place of a stitch – called a "starting chain", I rarely actually do them.

In Part 9 of the original Granny Square Academy, I introduced the option of the false stitch that I make in place of the starting chain. Doing this blends in so much better than your standard chain 3.

Here's a quick refresher of how it's done. You will see me doing this in the videos for the patterns.

*Pull up a long loop, a little taller than a normal stitch.*

*Place a finger on the loop on the hook and hold it firmly while moving the hook under, and wrapping the long loop around the hook.*

*Yarn over and pull that yarn-over under the wrapped long loop.*

*Yarn over again and pull through all remaining loops on the hook.*

It is most commonly used instead of chain 3 at the start of a round, but you can use it to replace any starting chain length. We'll explore that further in later parts.

When you join into a false stitch at the end of the round, you treat it as if you were working into a real stitch. You join to the part that is mimicking the top of a regular stitch. You will see that the "v" is made with one strand of yarn. If you pull the front strand of the "v" the back one disappears. I tend to use my fingernail to insert my hook under each strand of the "v".

This technique comes easy to some, while it may take several attempts to get for others. Here are my tips for making false stitches:

- Don't look at it in isolation. Yes, it will look weird on its own, but once you make some more stitches and then join into it, it looks so much like a real stitch!
- Pop a stitch marker in the top of it as soon as you make it, to show where to join into at the end of the round.

If you're not going to use false stitches, be mindful of joining into just the top single strand of the chain to make your starting chain look a little more like a real stitch as we did in the first Granny Square Academy.

## NOTE

When you need to start with chain 2 for a starting chain, replicating a half stitch, don't try to make a false stitch. Chain 2 per the pattern as it is too fiddly to do. It is a small stitch, so joining into the top strand of the second chain replicates a half stitch just fine.

Just like the magic circle, working a false stitch instead of the stated starting chains is optional. If you don't see starting chains as standing out in your finished work, it's totally fine to do the starting chains as the patterns say.

## NOTE

A false stitch is different to a standing stitch. Standing stitches are covered in Part 4.

# Other places to work a stitch

Let's begin by refreshing our understanding of the anatomy of crochet stitches.

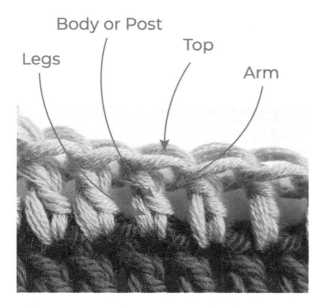

Legs • Body or Post • Top • Arm

Most often when crocheting, you poke your hook into the stitch under the "v" at the top. Think of the most common crochet stitch as a capital P (reversed for left-handers). That's where you insert your hook – into the circle part of the P. It's the same when working into other stitches – smaller, larger, clusters etc. It's the hole in the stitch on the right. (Left for left-handed folks.)

That's just one place you can work a stitch into a stitch. There are lots of other places you can poke your hook. In the first Granny Square Academy, I taught this with the front post and back post patterns, working around the posts of stitches, instead of into them. We also covered using the blo - back loop only where you only use the single back strand of the "v".

In our Part 1 pattern, we'll explore another place you can work a stitch in detail, the loop behind the "v".

## Loop Behind V

The "lbv" or "loop behind v" is an interesting place to work stitches into. I love this technique. It can be fiddly to do until you are used to it.

How it works is instead of working into the "v" of a stitch as you normally would, you work into the loop behind that "v". This strand of yarn is also known as the back bump or third loop. "Loop behind v" describes it best for me.

My Manderley patterns feature this technique a lot. It's what gives the flat edges of the flowers in the squares.

## Why do it?

I love the look it gives. Using the "loop behind v" leaves the "v" of the stitch of the previous round visible, but in a flat way. Sure, you can do back post stitches that leave that "v" visible, but that gives a thicker texture, and the base of the back post stitch is visible on the front of the work. While it is very similar, I would not use a back post instead if a pattern says lbv. They're generally not interchangeable. They give different effects as you see here.

*The square on the right was made with back posts instead of into loop behind v, and so it is smaller and bulkier.*

Not only is the effect different, stitches worked into the lbv are slightly taller than stitches worked as back posts.

My intention with this pattern was to have a flat middle section between the front post stitches.

**TIP**

**Practice! Really, the more you do the better you'll get at it and you will find it gets easier. Some folks use a smaller hook to find the lbv. If you do this, remember to change back to your regular one when back to normal stitch in stitch work.**

It is relatively easy to find and work into the lbv of half stitches. But you can use it, albeit with a little more effort on other stitches. I have been kind to you and only used half stitches in our lbv pattern.

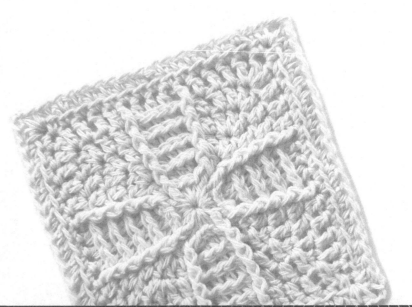

# Corners

If you're fresh from Granny Square Academy, you may recall that all patterns had 2-chain corner spaces when they were square.

That's not the only way to make corners. Sure, all the patterns in this book have 2-chain corner spaces in the final round, but in earlier rounds, many of them don't. Even though they are square.

I have kept the final round for all patterns as 2-chain corner spaces for two reasons. The first is so you can easily join them to the first Granny Square Academy patterns. The second is that 2-chain corners on the last round give a nice crisp corner. I like it better than all stitch corners in the last round.

> ## NOTE
>
> **You can join to squares which have stitches as corners – use the middle stitch as you would a 2-chain corner space when joining.**

In our first pattern, you will see corners which are described in the stitch counts as "3-st cnrs", for example. Corner stitches for the following round are worked into the middle stitch of those corner stitches.

Why? It makes for a more solid granny square. No gaps in the corners of the square!

*Stitch corners vs chain corners*

Just like rounds that have 2-chain corner spaces, you begin rounds in the middle of the corner and finish that first corner at the end of the round. The last stitch/es of the round are worked into the same stitch as the first of the round - i.e. the same stitch the slip stitch was made into.

Instead of joining with a stitch as you do with 2-chain corner spaces, you join with a slip stitch to your starting chain or false stitch.

*Same st as ss*

*Same st as first sts*

# Blocking

Blocking is a good idea as I discussed in the first Granny Square Academy. You will find it even more useful when making the patterns in this collection.

The greater variation of stitches and techniques used in the patterns means a greater chance you will find small size differences between the patterns, as well as the chance of a swirl happening. I'll talk more about why that is the case in the next part, but for now, know that blocking is a quick way to help even out size and a slight swirl.

This is the Part 1 pattern, blocked and unblocked.

Here's a quick revision of how I do it.

## Steam Blocking

I have a large foam mat that I have ruled 1-inch lines on.

I use these lines as a guide to pin out my squares. I start with the corners and then, depending on the pattern, add more along the sides. If there is a bit of a swirl I also straighten the centre and add pins inside the square.

I squirt the square with steam from my iron, making sure the iron does not touch the pins or yarn. (Yes, you can use a garment steamer or anything that shoots steam.)

I leave it to cool and dry and that's it. Done.

Your yarn fibre will impact how well this works. I use mostly 100% cotton yarns, so it works a treat.

It works well on cotton/bamboo blends and linen. I have blocked acrylic yarn squares this way as well.

It works to a lesser extent on pure wool. Sometimes, I also squirt wool squares with water and hover the hot, steamy iron over them. It's enough blocking to join, but I usually wet block my final project as well, if it's made with pure wool.

## Wet Blocking

You can wet block your squares as you make them, but it is more time consuming, so I usually leave it until I have a finished item.

Wash your item following the instructions for your yarn. For pure wool, that usually means, gently squishing the item in tepid water that has wool wash added. After soaking for ten to fifteen minutes, gently squeeze out the water. Lay it on towels and roll it up, squeezing as you go to remove more water. Repeat if needed. Lay out flat, pin the edges and leave to dry. I have many foam mats I pin to.

> **NOTE**
>
> **If you're brave, pop it in the washing machine for a spin cycle to remove water before laying flat.**

# Look Behind
# Vivien

## Part One · UK Pattern

## Abbreviations

| | | |
|---|---|---|
| | cnr | corner |
| | R | Round |
| | rep | repeat |
| | sp/s | space/s |
| | st/s | stitch/es |
| | stch | starting chain |
| • | ss | slip stitch |
| ○ | ch | chain |
| † | dc | double crochet |
| T | htr | half treble crochet |
| T | tr | treble crochet |
| U | fp | front post |
| ∨ | lbv | loop behind v |
| ∩ | blo | back loop only |

**Begin with mc.**

**R1:** ch3 (stch), *3htr**, (tr, ch2, tr)*, rep from * to * 2x and * to ** 1x, tr, ch1, join with dc to 3rd ch of stch.
{5 sts on each side; 4 2-ch cnr sps}

**R2:** ch3 (stch), *fptr around next st, htr in lbv of next 3 sts, fptr around next st**, tr in 2-ch cnr sp*, rep from * to * 2x and * to ** 1x, join with ss to 3rd ch of stch.
{5 sts on each side; 4 1-st cnrs}

**R3:** ch3 (stch), tr in same st as ss, *fptr around next st, htr in lbv of next 3 sts, fptr around next st**, 3tr in next st*, rep from * to * 2x and * to ** 1x, tr in same st as first sts, join with ss to 3rd ch of stch.
{5 sts on each side; 4 3-st cnrs}

**R4:** ch3 (stch), tr in same st as ss, *tr in next st, fptr around next st, htr in lbv of next 3 sts, fptr around next st, tr in next st**, 3tr in next st*, rep from * to * 2x and * to ** 1x, tr in same st as first sts, join with ss to 3rd ch of stch.
{7 sts on each side; 4 3-st cnrs}

**R5:** ch3 (stch), tr in same st as ss, *tr in next 2 sts, fptr around next st, htr in lbv of next 3 sts, fptr around next st, tr in next 2 sts**, 3tr in next st*, rep from * to * 2x and * to ** 1x, tr in same st as first sts, join with ss to 3rd ch of stch.
{9 sts on each side; 4 3-st cnrs}

**R6:** ch3 (stch), tr in same st as ss, *tr in next 3 sts, fptr around next st, htr in lbv of next 3 sts, fptr around next st, tr in next 3 sts**, 3tr in next st*, rep from * to * 2x and * to ** 1x, tr in same st as first sts, join with ss to 3rd ch of stch.
{11 sts on each side; 4 3-st cnrs}

**R7:** dc in same st as ss, *dc in next 13 sts**, (dc, ch2, dc) in next st*, rep from * to * 2x and * to ** 1x, dc in same st as first st, ch1, join with dc to first st.
{15 sts on each side; 4 2-ch cnr sps}

**R8:** ch2 (stch), htr over joining dc, *htr in blo of next 15 sts**, (2htr, ch2, 2htr) in 2-ch cnr sp*, rep from * to * 2x and * to ** 1x, 2htr in same sp as first sts, ch2, join with ss to 2nd ch of stch. Fasten off.
{19 sts on each side; 4 2-ch cnr sps}

# Look Behind
# Vivien

## Part One · US Pattern

## Abbreviations

| | | |
|---|---|---|
| | cnr | corner |
| | R | Round |
| | rep | repeat |
| | sp/s | space/s |
| | st/s | stitch/es |
| | stch | starting chain |
| • | ss | slip stitch |
| o | ch | chain |
| + | sc | single crochet |
| T | hdc | half double crochet |
| T | dc | double crochet |
| ว | fp | front post |
| ∨ | lbv | loop behind v |
| ∩ | blo | back loop only |

Begin with mc.

**R1:** ch3 (stch), *3hdc**, (dc, ch2, dc)*, rep from * to * 2x and * to ** 1x, dc, ch1, join with sc to 3rd ch of stch.
{5 sts on each side; 4 2-ch cnr sps}

**R2:** ch3 (stch), *fpdc around next st, hdc in lbv of next 3 sts, fpdc around next st**, dc in 2-ch cnr sp*, rep from * to * 2x and * to ** 1x, join with ss to 3rd ch of stch.
{5 sts on each side; 4 1-st cnrs}

**R3:** ch3 (stch), dc in same st as ss, *fpdc around next st, hdc in lbv of next 3 sts, fpdc around next st**, 3dc in next st*, rep from * to * 2x and * to ** 1x, dc in same st as first sts, join with ss to 3rd ch of stch.
{5 sts on each side; 4 3-st cnrs}

**R4:** ch3 (stch), dc in same st as ss, *dc in next st, fpdc around next st, hdc in lbv of next 3 sts, fpdc around next st, dc in next st**, 3dc in next st*, rep from * to * 2x and * to ** 1x, dc in same st as first sts, join with ss to 3rd ch of stch.
{7 sts on each side; 4 3-st cnrs}

**R5:** ch3 (stch), dc in same st as ss, *dc in next 2 sts, fpdc around next st, hdc in lbv of next 3 sts, fpdc around next st, dc in next 2 sts**, 3dc in next st*, rep from * to * 2x and * to ** 1x, dc in same st as first sts, join with ss to 3rd ch of stch.
{9 sts on each side; 4 3-st cnrs}

**R6:** ch3 (stch), dc in same st as ss, *dc in next 3 sts, fpdc around next st, hdc in lbv of next 3 sts, fpdc around next st, dc in next 3 sts**, 3dc in next st*, rep from * to * 2x and * to ** 1x, dc in same st as first sts, join with ss to 3rd ch of stch.
{11 sts on each side; 4 3-st cnrs}

**R7:** sc in same st as ss, *sc in next 13 sts**, (sc, ch2, sc) in next st*, rep from * to * 2x and * to ** 1x, sc in same st as first st, ch1, join with sc to first st.
{15 sts on each side; 4 2-ch cnr sps}

**R8:** ch2 (stch), hdc over joining sc, *hdc in blo of next 15 sts**, (2hdc, ch2, 2hdc) in 2-ch cnr sp*, rep from * to * 2x and * to ** 1x, 2hdc in same sp as first sts, ch2, join with ss to 2nd ch of stch. Fasten off.
{19 sts on each side; 4 2-ch cnr sps}

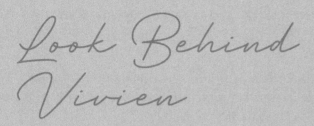

*Look Behind Vivien*

## Pattern Help

To maximize your learning, use these notes and photos to work from as you make the pattern.

If you get stuck, watch me make the pattern in the video:

 *Look Behind Vivien video*

 *Mirrored Look Behind Vivien video*

Prior knowledge needed from Granny Square Academy:

▷ *Working into stitches*
   **Part 1**

▷ *Joining with a stitch*
   **Part 1**

▷ *Working over joining stitch*
   **Part 1**

▷ *Using blo*
   **Part 3**

▷ *Making front post stitches*
   **Part 6**

# Round 1

Here's your chance to try the magic circle as well as the false stitch instead of chain 3 at the start. If you find it too fiddly as there is nothing much to hold on to, leave trying the false stitch until a later round.

Hold the base of your last stitch as you pull the tail tightly to close the magic circle before you join to the false stitch or 3rd chain of the starting chain.

# Round 2

Here's where you start using different parts of stitches to work into. After your starting chain or false stitch, the first stitch of the side is a front post stitch. This will be worked around the starting chain or false stitch of Round 1.

The middle 3 stitches of the side are all worked into the lbv of the half stitches from Round 1.

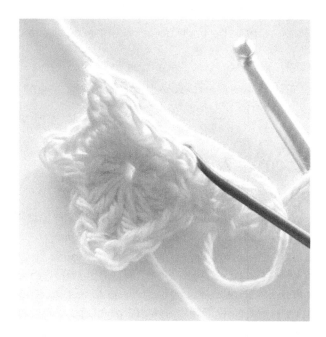

The last stitch of the side is another front post stitch and the corner in Round 2 is simply 1 stitch in the 2-chain corner space.

## Rounds 3 to 6

These rounds are practically the same. The middle 3 stitches of each side are always worked into the lbv. The only differences are:

- The corners are 3 stitches in 1 stitch, and
- There are from 1 to 3 stitches at the start and end of the sides.

## Round 7

A little refresher from GSA 1 for this round. As this is a small stitch round, pop a stitch marker in the first stitch as soon as you make it so it is easy to see where to join to at the end of the round. If you struggle to read small stitches, it's also a good idea to place a scrap of yarn in the gap before you join. This yarn scrap marks where to work the first and last stitches of Round 8.

## Round 8

In this round, you'll be using another place to work a stitch called the "back loop only" – blo for short.

Don't be concerned by the loop stretching. As you work more stitches, the loops settle.

## *Now...*

After you've made your first square, weave in your ends, block it and then make notes in the project planner. Record:

- Yarn and hook used
- Size
- Weight

Once you've done all of that, make another one or more. If you used the video, try to make it using the chart or written pattern this time. Note down how many more you make as you go.

Well done! Time to move on to the next lesson.

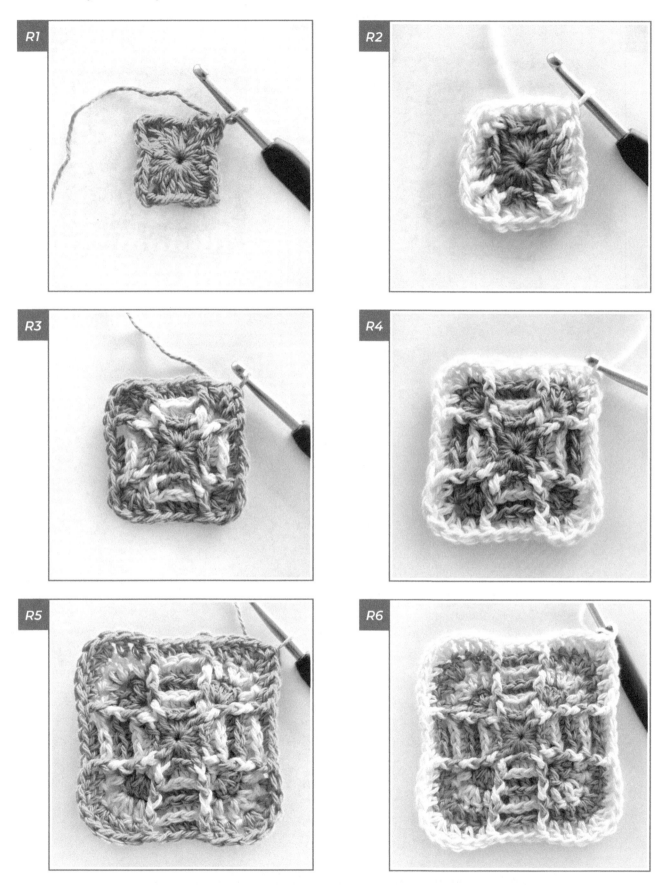

R1

R2

R3

R4

R5

R6

R7

R8

# Part Two

## Reading

## Patterns

## Tall Taylor Pattern Help

## Tall stitches

Tall stitches are not commonly used in small granny squares. Most often, you will find them in doilies, in lacier, light garments and accessories, and in large granny squares. Their use in granny squares is usually when squaring off circles and other shapes. Sometimes, they create surface texture when used as front post stitches into lower rounds.

Tall crochet stitches can be tricky!

Why though? Well, first, let's think about the number of steps there are when you make a regular crochet stitch as you would use in a traditional granny square.

*Yarn over, insert hook, pull up loop, yarn over, pull through two loops on hook, yarn over, pull through two loops on hook.*

That's a lot of steps – seven actions to create 1 stitch.

Now think about a tall, long stitch. There are even more steps! These are all the steps for the tall stitch I have used in the Tall Taylor pattern.

*Yarn over three times, insert hook, pull up a loop, yarn over, pull through two loops on hook, yarn over, pull through two loops on hook, yarn over, pull through two loops on hook, yarn over, pull through two loops on hook.*

Eleven actions for 1 stitch!

Every one of those steps is a chance for variation in stitch size.

**Some folks find their tall stitches very loose and floppy. If you find this is the case, try tugging gently on your yarn after each yarn over and pull through two loops on hook.**

This is why granny squares can turn out a different size. If you make your crochet stitches in even a slightly different way to the designer of the pattern, you can get a different size than you expected.

Let's explore that further.

I made each of these four circles using tall stitches. I used the same yarn and the same hook to make them all. And yet, they vary in size considerably.

Most of the difference comes from when you insert your hook into a stitch or space and pull up a loop.

For the largest circle, I pulled the loop up higher than the previous round's stitches and was very loose with my tension as I crocheted. This is called "lifting".

For the smallest circle, I pulled the loop to the front of the previous round, not lifting it at all. I then was very tight with my tension, tugging the yarn a lot as I made each step of the stitch. This is called "yanking".

The two middle-sized ones are very similar. One is where I pulled the loop until my hook was level horizontally with the top of the previous round's stitches. This is called "riding" and is the ideal method, as the loop on the hook is the diameter of your hook and so creates the ideal sized stitch.

The last one is how I naturally crochet. I do a combination of lifting and yanking, without thought, as I crochet. You may find you do one or more of these styles in combination as well.

# Crochet gauge

How you crochet is a big contributor to your crochet gauge. Gauge is the size your work should turn out to be, often listed in patterns. But as you can see, there are so many opportunities for difference, even in a simple pattern. With granny squares, it generally doesn't matter. If your blanket, scarf, cowl is a little smaller or larger than the pattern says, it will still work just fine.

Where it does become an issue is when you are making fitted garments. In that case, it is important to match the designer's gauge. And here's where that can be tricky! If you are a knitter, you may be used to matching gauge. As there are so few steps in the common knit/purl stitches, if your gauge is off, you can usually change your needle size to match the pattern's gauge.

It's not so simple with crochet. You may find you match the horizonal gauge just fine, but your vertical gauge is very different or vice versa. Changing your hook size will not fix that.

Instead, you will have to either alter your crochet style to make your stitches shorter or taller, or alter the pattern to do more or less rows or rounds. Neither of these things is easy. Mindfully working each stitch differently to your natural crochet style is hard. And adding or removing rounds to a fitted pattern is difficult!

As we are in granny square world, it's not much of an issue, thankfully.

## What to do about size differences

You may find, because of the possible variation in different stitches used, that some of your squares you make from this book are a slightly different size.

You can easily deal with this by blocking to size if it's a small difference, or adding a round or two of small stitches if the difference is larger.

# Using a false stitch for tall stitches

If you've been using the false stitch in place of the chain 3 starting chain at the beginning of rounds, you may have had the thought, but what about when I need to chain 4 or 5 for a starting chain?
Can I make a false stitch then?

Absolutely you can use a false stitch instead. All you do is pull up a longer loop and wrap that long loop more times depending on the stitch type you are replicating. You wrap twice instead of chain 4 and three times instead of chain 5.

It will look even weirder than the chain 3 false stitch, but once you join into it, it will look much better. You will see me making these false stitches in the videos.

# Blocking the swirl

In your granny square adventures, you may have come across a pattern that while it's square, the centre section is swirly. I'll talk about why that happens in detail in Part 5. You will find it happens in the pattern I have for you for this part.

In this case, most of the swirl is part of the cool look of the pattern, highlighting those tall stitches. But the centre section is meant to be square and straight. Blocking is where you can straighten it up. This goes for any pattern.

After you have pinned out the edges of your square, use your fingers to twist the swirly part and pop some pins in here and there and block as normal.

## Tall Taylor

### Part Two · UK Pattern

## Abbreviations

| | |
|---|---|
| cnr | corner |
| R | Round |
| rep | repeat |
| sp/s | space/s |
| st/s | stitch/es |
| stch | starting chain |
| • ss | slip stitch |
| ○ ch | chain |
| + dc | double crochet |
| T tr | treble crochet |
| ⊤ ttr | triple treble crochet |
| V spike | spike stitch |

Begin with mc.

**R1:** ch3 (stch), 2tr, *ch2, 3tr*, rep from * to * 2x, ch1, join with dc to 3rd ch of stch.
{3 sts on each side; 4 2-ch cnr sps}

**R2:** dc over joining dc, *dc in next 3 sts**, (dc, ch2, dc) in 2-ch cnr sp*, rep from * to * 2x and * to ** 1x, dc in same sp as first st, ch1, join with dc to first st.
{5 sts on each side; 4 2-ch cnr sps}

**R3:** ch5 (stch), ch1, ttr over joining dc, *ttr in next 5 sts**, (2x [ttr, ch1], ttr) in 2-ch cnr sp*, rep from * to * 2x and * to ** 1x, ttr in same sp as first sts, ch1, join with ss to 5th ch of stch.
{7 sts, 2 1-ch sps on each side; 4 1-st cnrs}

**R4:** dc in same st as ss, *dc in 1-ch sp, dc in next 7 sts, dc in 1-ch sp**, (dc, ch2, dc) in next st*, rep from * to * 2x and * to ** 1x, dc in same st as first st, ch1, join with dc to first st.
{11 sts on each side; 4 2-ch cnr sps}

**R5:** ch3 (stch), tr over joining dc, *tr in next 11 sts**, (2tr, ch2, 2tr) in 2-ch cnr sp*, rep from * to * 2x and * to ** 1x, 2tr in same sp as first sts, ch1, join with dc to 3rd ch of stch.
{15 sts on each side; 4 2-ch cnr sps}

**R6:** dc over joining dc, *dc in next 15 sts**, (dc, ch2, dc) in 2-ch cnr sp*, rep from * to * 2x and * to ** 1x, dc in same sp as first st, ch1, join with dc to first st.
{17 sts on each side; 4 2-ch cnr sps}

**R7:** dc over joining dc, *8x [ch1, skip 1 st, dc in next st], ch1, skip 1 st**, (dc, ch2, dc) in 2-ch cnr sp*, rep from * to * 2x and * to ** 1x, dc in same sp as first st, ch1, join with dc to first st.
{10 sts, 9 1-ch sps on each side; 4 2-ch cnr sps}

**R8:** dc over joining dc, *9x [dc in next st, spike dc over 1-ch sp into skipped st of R6], dc in next st**, (dc, ch2, dc) in 2-ch cnr sp*, rep from * to * 2x and * to ** 1x, dc in same sp as first st, ch2, join with ss to first st. Fasten off.
{21 sts on each side; 4 2-ch cnr sps}

# Tall Taylor

## Part Two · US Pattern

## Abbreviations

| | | |
|---|---|---|
| | cnr | corner |
| | R | Round |
| | rep | repeat |
| | sp/s | space/s |
| | st/s | stitch/es |
| | stch | starting chain |
| • | ss | slip stitch |
| ○ | ch | chain |
| + | sc | single crochet |
| T | dc | double crochet |
| ‡ | dtr | double triple crochet |
| V | spike | spike stitch |

Begin with mc.

**R1:** ch3 (stch), 2dc, *ch2, 3dc*, rep from * to * 2x, ch1, join with sc to 3rd ch of stch.
{3 sts on each side; 4 2-ch cnr sps}

**R2:** sc over joining sc, *sc in next 3 sts**, (sc, ch2, sc) in 2-ch cnr sp*, rep from * to * 2x and * to ** 1x, sc in same sp as first st, ch1, join with sc to first st.
{5 sts on each side; 4 2-ch cnr sps}

**R3:** ch5 (stch), ch1, dtr over joining sc, *dtr in next 5 sts**, (2x [dtr, ch1], dtr) in 2-ch cnr sp*, rep from * to * 2x and * to ** 1x, dtr in same sp as first sts, ch1, join with ss to 5th ch of stch.
{7 sts, 2 1-ch sps on each side; 4 1-st cnrs}

**R4:** sc in same st as ss, *sc in 1-ch sp, sc in next 7 sts, sc in 1-ch sp**, (sc, ch2, sc) in next st*, rep from * to * 2x and * to ** 1x, sc in same st as first st, ch1, join with sc to first st.
{11 sts on each side; 4 2-ch cnr sps}

**R5:** ch3 (stch), dc over joining sc, *dc in next 11 sts**, (2dc, ch2, 2dc) in 2-ch cnr sp*, rep from * to * 2x and * to ** 1x, 2dc in same sp as first sts, ch1, join with sc to 3rd ch of stch.
{15 sts on each side; 4 2-ch cnr sps}

**R6:** sc over joining sc, *sc in next 15 sts**, (sc, ch2, sc) in 2-ch cnr sp*, rep from * to * 2x and * to ** 1x, sc in same sp as first st, ch1, join with sc to first st.
{17 sts on each side; 4 2-ch cnr sps}

**R7:** sc over joining sc, *8x [ch1, skip 1 st, sc in next st], ch1, skip 1 st**, (sc, ch2, sc) in 2-ch cnr sp*, rep from * to * 2x and * to ** 1x, sc in same sp as first st, ch1, join with sc to first st.
{10 sts, 9 1-ch sps on each side; 4 2-ch cnr sps}

**R8:** sc over joining sc, *9x [sc in next st, spike sc over 1-ch sp into skipped st of R6], sc in next st**, (sc, ch2, sc) in 2-ch cnr sp*, rep from * to * 2x and * to ** 1x, sc in same sp as first st, ch2, join with ss to first st. Fasten off.
{21 sts on each side; 4 2-ch cnr sps}

# Tall Taylor

## Pattern Help

To maximize your learning, use these notes and photos to work from as you make the pattern.

If you get stuck, watch me make the pattern in the video:

*Tall Taylor video*

*Mirrored Tall Taylor video*

Prior knowledge needed from Granny Square Academy:

▷ *Skipping stitches* **Part 2**

▷ *Spike stitches* **Part 4**

Easy rounds are not referred to from here on in, only the ones that may need a little more explaining.

# Round 3

After the first two easy rounds, Round 3 is where we try most of the new things.

All the stitches of Round 3 are tall stitches, and the corners are made up of 3 stitches separated by 1-chain spaces.

The first tall stitch, after your chain 5 or false stitch is worked over the joining stitch. Use the tips for small stitch rounds mentioned in Part 1 to make it easy to see where to work your first corner stitches.

Remember to chain 1 before you join with a slip stich at the end of the round.

Don't be alarmed at the floppiness at the end of this round. To help with the next round, finger block your square, pulling from each middle corner stitch and it will look much better.

*Red needle shows where to work the first and last stitches of Round 3*

## Round 4

There's nothing hard about this round as you are working a stitch in every stitch and chain space along the sides, and we have the common 2-chain space corners from here on in. This round of small stitches will square up your shape nicely.

## Round 8

The last round uses spike stitches to fill the gaps formed by the chain 1, skip 1 stitch in Round 7. Work your spike stitch into the skipped Round 6 stitch, skipped in Round 7, over the 1-chain spaces.

The first spike stitch is worked into the first stitch of Round 6, over the 1-chain space of Round 7.

As you move along the side, you are alternating between working into Round 6 and 7 stitches.

## Now...

After you've made your first square, weave in your ends, block it and then make notes in the project planner. Record:

- Yarn and hook used
- Size
- Weight

Once you've done all of that, make another one or more. If you used the video, try to make it using the chart or written pattern this time. Note down how many more you make as you go.

Well done! Time to move on to the next lesson.

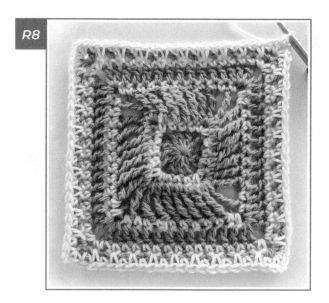

# Part Three

## Reading

## Patterns

## Billie Between Pattern Help

## Working between stitches

As you know, most often you will work into the hole to the right of a stitch (left for left-handers). Sometimes, patterns also instruct you to work between stitches. It is a very small thing, but it really does give a very different effect.

What you see here are two solid granny squares, one made working into stitches as usual, and the other made by working between stitches. The stitch count of the patterns is slightly different as it is not possible to work the same number of stitches into stitches as when working between stitches.

There is also a visible difference as you can see. Not only is the "between stitches" square swirly, it is also significantly smaller than the "into stitches" square. And there are gaps between the stitches, whereas the regular one is quite solid.

In     Between

So, when do you work between stitches?

Working between stitches can be used to add a stitch (an increase), define other stitches like clusters or make some space. It's not common to work between stitches for a whole round in a granny square.

## Last stitch/next stitch?

When you get to an instruction to work between stitches, at first glance it may confuse. Let's break it down.

In my patterns, I like to dictate what happens to every stitch in the previous round. That means every stitch will be referenced either as worked into or to be skipped. Most commonly, the patterns will state something like, "dc in next st". That means that you work a dc into the next stitch. Nothing new there.

But when you are to work between stitches, depending on the pattern, there are a couple of ways to express it.

The first way is if stitches are to be worked into as well as have stitches worked between them.

> *"... dc in next st, dc between last and next sts, ..."*

In this instance, firstly you work a dc into the stitch (your next stitch). It has now been used, so it is now the last stitch. Then you work a stitch between the one just used and the next one that is still unused. i.e. between last and next stitches.

*Needle on right: last stitch, red needle: between stitches, needle on left: next stitch*

········································

**TIP**

**Working between stitches can obscure the hole in the next stitch, so be mindful of that if you need to work into it.**

The next way to express working between stitches is if the stitches are only being worked between and not into at all.

*"... dc between next 2 sts, ..."*

*Silver needle: last stitch, red needle: between next 2*

This means you are not working into any stitches, but between the next 2 stitches. 2 stitches have been referenced and so there is no need to specify to skip any. If this kind of instruction was to be written like in the first instance, it'd be longer:

*"... skip next st, dc between last and next st, skip next st, ..."*

Both types of instruction are used in the Billie Between pattern so you can get an understanding of how it all works. This pattern is one where making it really helps to understand the instructions.

# Billie Between

## Part Three · UK Pattern

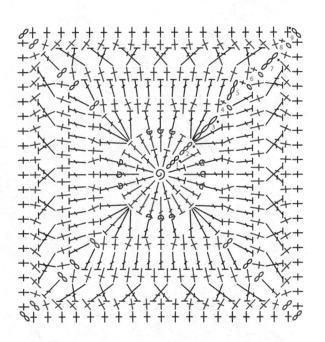

## Abbreviations

| | | |
|---|---|---|
| | cnr | corner |
| | R | Round |
| | rep | repeat |
| | sp/s | space/s |
| | st/s | stitch/es |
| | stch | starting chain |
| • | ss | slip stitch |
| o | ch | chain |
| + | dc | double crochet |
| T | tr | treble crochet |
| c | bp | back post |

Begin with mc.

**R1:** ch3 (stch), 11tr, join with ss to 3rd ch of stch.
{12 sts}

**R2:** ch3 (stch), tr between same st as ss and next st, *tr in next st, tr between last and next sts*, rep from * to * 10x, join with ss to 3rd ch of stch.
{24 sts}

**R3:** ch3 (stch), 2tr in same st as ss, *skip 1 st, bptr around next 3 sts, skip 1 st**, 5tr in next st*, rep from * to * 2x and * to ** 1x, 2tr in same st as first sts, join with ss to 3rd ch of stch.
{3 sts on each side; 4 5-st cnrs}

**R4:** dc in same st as ss, *dc in next 2 sts, dc between last and next sts, dc in next 3 sts, dc between last and next sts, dc in next 2 sts**, (dc, ch2, dc) in next st*, rep from * to * 2x and * to ** 1x, dc in same st as first st, ch1, join with dc to first st.
{11 sts on each side; 4 2-ch cnr sps}

**R5:** ch3 (stch), *tr in next 11 sts**, (tr, ch2, tr) in 2-ch cnr sp*, rep from * to * 2x and * to ** 1x, tr in same sp as first st, ch1, join with dc to 3rd ch of stch.
{13 sts on each side; 4 2-ch cnr sps}

**R6:** dc over joining dc, *12x [dc between next 2 sts], skip next st**, (dc, ch2, dc) in 2-ch cnr sp*, rep from * to * 2x and * to ** 1x, dc in same sp as first st, ch1, join with dc to first st.
{14 sts on each side; 4 2-ch cnr sps}

**R7:** ch3 (stch), *7x [skip 1 st, tr in next st, tr in skipped st]**, tr in 2-ch cnr sp*, rep from * to * 2x and * to ** 1x, join with ss to 3rd ch of stch.
{14 sts on each side; 4 1-st cnrs}

**R8:** dc in same st as ss, *dc between last and next sts, 14x [dc between next 2 sts]**, (dc, ch2, dc) in next st*, rep from * to * 2x and * to ** 1x, dc in same st as first st, ch1, join with dc to first st.
{17 sts on each side; 4 2-ch cnr sps}

**R9:** dc over joining dc, *dc in next 17 sts**, (dc, ch2, dc) in 2-ch cnr sp*, rep from * to * 2x and * to ** 1x, dc in same sp as first st, ch2, join with ss to first st. Fasten off.
{19 sts on each side; 4 2-ch cnr sps}

# Billie Between

## Part Three · US Pattern

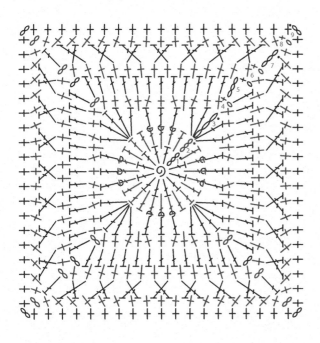

## Abbreviations

| | | |
|---|---|---|
| | cnr | corner |
| | R | Round |
| | rep | repeat |
| | sp/s | space/s |
| | st/s | stitch/es |
| | stch | starting chain |
| • | ss | slip stitch |
| ○ | ch | chain |
| + | sc | single crochet |
| † | dc | double crochet |
| ͻ | bp | back post |

Begin with mc.

**R1:** ch3 (stch), 11dc, join with ss to 3rd ch of stch.
{12 sts}

**R2:** ch3 (stch), dc between same st as ss and next st, *dc in next st, dc between last and next sts*, rep from * to * 10x, join with ss to 3rd ch of stch.
{24 sts}

**R3:** ch3 (stch), 2dc in same st as ss, *skip 1 st, bpdc around next 3 sts, skip 1 st**, 5dc in next st*, rep from * to * 2x and * to ** 1x, 2dc in same st as first sts, join with ss to 3rd ch of stch.
{3 sts on each side; 4 5-st cnrs}

**R4:** sc in same st as ss, *sc in next 2 sts, sc between last and next sts, sc in next 3 sts, sc between last and next sts, sc in next 2 sts**, (sc, ch2, sc) in next st*, rep from * to * 2x and * to ** 1x, sc in same st as first st, ch1, join with sc to first st.
{11 sts on each side; 4 2-ch cnr sps}

**R5:** ch3 (stch), *dc in next 11 sts**, (dc, ch2, dc) in 2-ch cnr sp*, rep from * to * 2x and * to ** 1x, dc in same sp as first st, ch1, join with sc to 3rd ch of stch.
{13 sts on each side; 4 2-ch cnr sps}

**R6:** sc over joining sc, *12x [sc between next 2 sts], skip next st**, (sc, ch2, sc) in 2-ch cnr sp*, rep from * to * 2x and * to ** 1x, sc in same sp as first st, ch1, join with sc to first st.
{14 sts on each side; 4 2-ch cnr sps}

**R7:** ch3 (stch), *7x [skip 1 st, dc in next st, dc in skipped st]**, dc in 2-ch cnr sp*, rep from * to * 2x and * to ** 1x, join with ss to 3rd ch of stch.
{14 sts on each side; 4 1-st cnrs}

**R8:** sc in same st as ss, *sc between last and next sts, 14x [sc between next 2 sts]**, (sc, ch2, sc) in next st*, rep from * to * 2x and * to ** 1x, sc in same st as first st, ch1, join with sc to first st.
{17 sts on each side; 4 2-ch cnr sps}

**R9:** sc over joining sc, *sc in next 17 sts**, (sc, ch2, sc) in 2-ch cnr sp*, rep from * to * 2x and * to ** 1x, sc in same sp as first st, ch2, join with ss to first st. Fasten off.
{19 sts on each side; 4 2-ch cnr sps}

Pattern Help

To maximize your learning, use these notes and photos to work from as you make the pattern.

If you get stuck, watch me make the pattern in the video:

*Billie Between video*

*Mirrored Billie Between video*

Prior knowledge needed from Granny Square Academy:

▷ *Anatomy of a stitch*
**Part 1**

▷ *Skipping stitches*
**Part 2**

▷ *Making back post stitches*
**Part 5**

## Round 2

There is a stitch worked between every stitch as well as a stitch worked into each stitch. You may have to move aside your stitch worked between to find the stitch to work into.

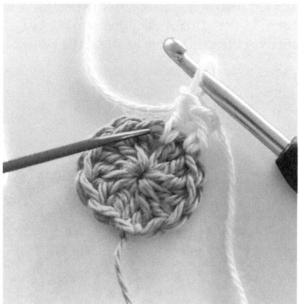

## Round 3

Nothing too tricky in this round. The corners are made by working 5 stitches in one. Along the sides, you are skipping a stitch at the start and end, working back post stitches around the 3 middle stitches. The needles in the photo show the skipped stitches.

## Round 4

You'll be working between stitches in this round, just like you did in Round 2, but this time, you're not working between every stitch. You are working a stitch between stitches either side of the 3 back post stitches.

## Round 6

Once more, you will be working between stitches. The instruction reads differently though as this time, you are not working into stitches at all, only between them.

The last instruction for each side says to "skip next st". That means you skip the last stitch of the side before working the corner.

The corners are worked into the 2-chain corner spaces.

The thing to watch out for is reading the stitches correctly when skipping the next stitch, as it can look like the stitch used for the first stitch of the cross hasn't been used.

## Round 7

This round is all about skipping stitches and also using those same skipped stitches, creating cool cross shapes.

What you are doing is skipping a stitch, working a stitch in the next stitch, then working a stitch in the one you just skipped. It does feel a little awkward at first, but you soon get used to it.

*Red needle shows the next stitch to be skipped and the silver needle, the next stitch to be worked into.*

# Round 8

This round is essentially the same as Round 6, but the instructions read a little differently, as the corners in the last round are 1-stitch corners. This means the first instruction is referring to the corner stitch as the last stitch.

The needles show where the first 2 stitches are worked. It may be a little trickier when working between the crossed stitches, but the method is the same.

The last stitch before the corner is worked between the last 2 stitches of the side.

And the last round is an easy one. You can do it.

## Now...

After you've made your first square, weave in your ends, block it and then make notes in the project planner. Record:

- Yarn and hook used
- Size
- Weight

Once you've done all of that, make another one or more. If you used the video, try to make it using the chart or written pattern this time. Note down how many more you make as you go.

Well done! Time to move on to the next lesson.

# Part Four

## Reading

## Patterns

## Invisible Jesse Pattern Help

## Why use an invisible join?

In my opinion, there are only a few instances where using an invisible join is necessary.

There is no need for an invisible join if a stitch with a slip stitch join is going to be worked into in a solid kind of pattern. The slip stitch join will be hidden.

That goes for the join of the last round of a granny square too, if you are using a "use every stitch" joining method, as the stitch joined into will be used.

### EXCEPTION

Of course, there is always an exception to any rule. If you are joining your granny squares together with a join that only uses the back loops of the granny squares (like the zipper join on page 175). In that case, an invisible join would make the joining of squares neater.

## So when do you use it?

The main instance is when the edge of a round of stitches will be seen in full. It creates an unbroken line of the little "v's" on top of crochet stitches.

The only other time I sometimes use an invisible join is when making the good old circle in a square. And only sometimes. It all depends on the yarn used. If it's a not-fluffy, smoother yarn, joining with an invisible join helps everything look even smoother.

*Carpentaria from Siren's Atlas*

The same is true if using the back loop only of stitches to leave a thin, solid line on the front. I joined a round part way through this pattern with an invisible join to create the unbroken circle you see.

*Red needle is pointing to a slip stitch join, silver needle is pointing to an invisible join*

Here's the comparison of the Invisible Jesse pattern made with slip stitch joins and invisible joins. As you can see, the one on the right is more visually pleasing with the unbroken lines of stitches.

*Left: slip stitch join, right: invisible join*

## Special note!

You'll see in the pattern that I start the rounds to be ended with an invisible join with this note:

> ### Don't work a false st

Why not? I usually recommend it for a seamless look. Well, the aim of using the invisible join is to mimic a real stitch. The starting chain together with the invisible join replicate a stitch very closely. If you start with a false stitch, the invisible join creates a second "v" on the top of the false stitch that adds extra bulk that will stand out.

## How to make an invisible join

Here are the steps to make an invisible join:

1. Cut yarn and pull the tail up through last stitch made.

2. Thread tail onto yarn needle and insert it into the first true stitch of the round.

3. Insert yarn needle into the top of the last stitch where the yarn tail emerges from and the lbv of that stitch.

4. Pull tail until the loop you made is the same size as the "v's" of the other stitches of the round.

Let's look at each step.

### Cut yarn and pull up tail

You want to leave yourself enough of a tail to work with easily, so don't be skimpy with it. Once the yarn is cut, pull the loop on your hook up so the tail emerges from the top of the last stitch you made. This means the tail is emerging from the middle of the v of the last stitch of the round.

## Thread end onto your yarn needle and insert

Now, you need to look for the first true stitch of the round. Remember how I said I want you to make the starting chain and not a false stitch? That means the first stitch after your starting chain is the first true stitch. It's not the chain 3 pretending to be a stitch, it is the first real stitch.

Once you have identified the stitch, insert your yarn needle under the "v" just like you would insert your hook if you were working into it.

*Silver needle is pointing to the top of 3rd chain of the starting chain, and the red needle first true stitch*

## Insert yarn needle into top of last stitch and lbv

Look for the place the yarn tail is emerging from. That is where you insert the yarn needle, back into the top of the last stitch of the round, making sure you also go into the lbv.

## Pull tail

Now it's a matter of pulling the tail until the loop you have just made is the same size as the tops of the other stitches in the round.

## Ends

Let's talk about ends! Yes, there are a lot of ends in the Invisible Jesse pattern. That's the price you pay for using invisible joins. It doesn't have to be a chore though. I weave in the ends a little bit as I make the join and finish them off when I finish each square.

I don't fully weave in the end as I make the invisible join. There are a couple of reasons. The first is that it can make it hard to work the next round's stitches if you need to work in the lbv as we did in Part 1, or if you need to make post stitches.

The second reason is, sometimes the next round can mess with your invisible join, pulling it tighter or making it looser. If you leave weaving in the end until the end of the square, you can more easily adjust the invisible join as you secure the end properly.

As this pattern is a solid one, you can crochet over the ends from your standing stitches as you go. I recommend that you change direction at least once or twice when weaving in ends. Crocheting over them saves you one step of the weaving process.

## Why are you not finishing in the middle of a corner?

When following seamless crochet methods, you start and end rounds in the middle of a corner.

You only need to finish in the middle of a corner when you are continuing with the same colour in the next round, and you are not ending the colour. As making an invisible join involves cutting your yarn, it is not necessary to start and end in the middle of a corner.

## *Standing stitches*

This is a great way to attach your yarn after ending with an invisible join (or changing colour). You can't get more seamless than starting with a real stitch! Nothing pretending or taking the place of a stitch.

Standing stitches were covered a little in the first Granny Square Academy with the Circle Cindy pattern. Let's look at them a little more closely.

You make a standing stitch by attaching your yarn to your hook with a slip knot and making the stitch required. The only thing that is different, is you need to keep a finger on the loop on your hook as you make the stitch or you will lose any yarn overs you need to do.

Any stitch can be made as a standing stitch. A cluster, a popcorn, a tall stitch, a small

stitch. In the pattern for this part, you will be instructed what stitch to make with a standing stitch.

But! You don't have to wait to be told what stitch to use. If you were making a pattern written for one colour, but wanted to change colours at any point, you can use a standing stitch instead of any starting chains a pattern may state.

For example, if I was starting a new colour in a round that began with ch3 (stch), instead, I would make a standing treble/double crochet (UK/US). If it said, ch4 (stch), I would start with a standing double treble/triple crochet (UK/US). If it began with "ch3 (stch), tr2tog in same st as ss", I would begin with a standing tr3tog/dc3tog (UK/US).

*Standing tr/dc (UK/US)*  *Standing tr3tog/ dc3tog (UK/US)*

## Joining to a standing stitch

When you join to a standing stitch, you can get quite a big gap if you're not careful. I have one little, tiny trick for you that will make you go "oooohhhh!".

When you insert your hook into the standing stitch, make sure your yarn over to make your joining stitch sits to the left of the slip knot of the standing stitch (right for left handers). Then, as you complete your join, you will see the slip knot disappear to the back and you won't have a big gap. Magic!

## Production line making

The Invisible Jessie pattern is a good one to try the production line method of making granny squares, if you plan on making more than one.

Make however many you need up to the end of Round 2, then add Rounds 3 and 4, then Rounds 5 and 6 before you finish them all off.

You really get to know the pattern well this way and it helps to commit it to memory.

The production line method of making is a great way to go if you're using a lot of colours too. It feels faster somehow.

### EXTRA PLAY

**Remake a Circle Cindy from the original Granny Square Academy using an invisible join in Round 3 to understand the difference to joining the circle with a slip stitch yourself.**

### NOTE

**A standing stitch is used to attach your yarn after cutting for an invisible join or changing colour. It is a real stitch.**

**A false stitch is used when the yarn is still attached and you are continuing the same colour. It is replicating a stitch and is done instead of a starting chain.**

# Invisible Jesse

## Part Four · UK Pattern

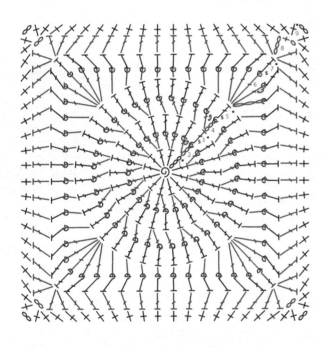

## Abbreviations

| | | |
|---|---|---|
| | cnr | corner |
| | R | Round |
| | rep | repeat |
| | sp/s | space/s |
| | st/s | stitch/es |
| | stch | starting chain |
| • | ss | slip stitch |
| o | ch | chain |
| + | dc | double crochet |
| T | htr | half treble crochet |
| T | tr | treble crochet |
| c | bp | back post |
| ⌒ | inv join | invisible join |
| s | stdg | standing |

Begin with mc.

**R1:** ch3 (stch), 11tr, join with ss to 3rd ch of stch.
{12 sts}

**R2:** Don't work a false stitch. ch3 (stch), tr in same st as ss, 2tr in next 11 sts, join with inv join to first true stitch.
{24 sts}

**R3:** Attach with stdg bptr to any st, bptr around next 23 sts, join with ss to first st.
{24 sts}

**R4:** Don't work a false stitch. ch3 (stch), tr in same st as ss, *tr in next st**, 2tr in next st*, rep from * to * 10x and * to ** 1x, join with inv join to first true stitch.
{36 sts}

**R5:** Attach with stdg bptr to any st, bptr around next 35 sts, join with ss to first st.
{36 sts}

**R6:** Don't work a false stitch. ch3 (stch), 4tr in same st as ss, *htr in next 8 sts**, 5tr in next st*, rep from * to * 2x and * to ** 1x, join with inv join to first true st.
{8 sts on each side; 4 5-st cnrs}

**R7:** Attach with stdg bptr to the middle st of any 5-st cnr, bptr around next st, *bphtr around next 10 sts**, bptr around next 3 sts*, rep from * to * 2x and * to ** 1x, bptr around next st, join with ss to first st.
{12 sts on each side; 4 1-st cnrs}

**R8:** ch3 (stch), tr in same st as ss, *tr in next 12 sts**, (2tr, ch2, 2tr) in next st*, rep from * to * 2x and * to ** 1x, 2tr in same st as first sts, ch1, join with dc to 3rd ch of stch.
{16 sts on each side; 4 2-ch cnr sps}

**R9:** 2dc over joining dc, *dc in next 16 sts**, (2dc, ch2, 2dc) in 2-ch cnr sp*, rep from * to * 2x and * to ** 1x, 2dc in same sp as first sts, ch2, join with ss to first st. Fasten off.
{20 sts on each side; 4 2-ch cnr sps}

# Invisible Jesse

## Part Four · US Pattern

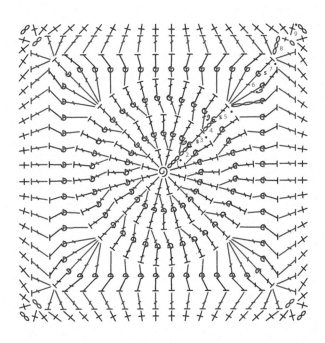

## Abbreviations

| | |
|---|---|
| cnr | corner |
| R | Round |
| rep | repeat |
| sp/s | space/s |
| st/s | stitch/es |
| stch | starting chain |
| ss | slip stitch |
| ch | chain |
| sc | single crochet |
| hdc | half double crochet |
| dc | double crochet |
| bp | back post |
| inv join | invisible join |
| stdg | standing |

Begin with mc.

**R1:** ch3 (stch), 11dc, join with ss to 3rd ch of stch.
{12 sts}

**R2:** Don't work a false stitch. ch3 (stch), dc in same st as ss, 2dc in next 11 sts, join with inv join to first true stitch.
{24 sts}

**R3:** Attach with stdg bpdc to any st, bpdc around next 23 sts, join with ss to first st.
{24 sts}

**R4:** Don't work a false stitch. ch3 (stch), dc in same st as ss, *dc in next st**, 2dc in next st*, rep from * to * 10x and * to ** 1x, join with inv join to first true stitch.
{36 sts}

**R5:** Attach with stdg bpdc to any st, bpdc around next 35 sts, join with ss to first st.
{36 sts}

**R6:** Don't work a false stitch. ch3 (stch), 4dc in same st as ss, *hdc in next 8 sts**, 5dc in next st*, rep from * to * 2x and * to ** 1x, join with inv join to first true st.
{8 sts on each side; 4 5-st cnrs}

**R7:** Attach with stdg bpdc to the middle st of any 5-st cnr, bpdc around next st, *bphdc around next 10 sts**, bpdc around next 3 sts*, rep from * to * 2x and * to ** 1x, bpdc around next st, join with ss to first st.
{12 sts on each side; 4 1-st cnrs}

**R8:** ch3 (stch), dc in same st as ss, *dc in next 12 sts**, (2dc, ch2, 2dc) in next st*, rep from * to * 2x and * to ** 1x, 2dc in same st as first sts, ch1, join with sc to 3rd ch of stch.
{16 sts on each side; 4 2-ch cnr sps}

**R9:** 2sc over joining sc, *sc in next 16 sts**, (2sc, ch2, 2sc) in 2-ch cnr sp*, rep from * to * 2x and * to ** 1x, 2sc in same sp as first sts, ch2, join with ss to first st. Fasten off.
{20 sts on each side; 4 2-ch cnr sps}

# Invisible Jesse

## Pattern Help

To maximize your learning, use these notes and photos to work from as you make the pattern.

If you get stuck, watch me make the pattern in the video:

*Invisible Jesse video*

*Mirrored Invisible Jesse video*

Prior knowledge needed from Granny Square Academy:

▷ *Anatomy of a stitch*
   **Part 1**

▷ *Making back post stitches*
   **Part 5**

## Round 2

A simple round, but make sure you start with the starting chain and not a false stitch so you can end with an invisible join.

## Round 3

This is an easy round, and you will use the same technique in Rounds 5 and 7. Pick any stitch and work a standing back post stitch around it and all other stitches of the round, remembering the joining to a standing stitch trick mentioned in the reading.

## Round 6

If you were continuing the same colour, the pattern would have you start with half of the first corner for a more seamless look. However, as the round is ending with an invisible join, there is no need to end in the middle of a corner. The first corner is made with all 5 stitches, but the first is a chain 3 starting chain.

## Round 7

This round is very similar to the other back post rounds, but as well as creating the raised rounded square shape, we are completing the squaring off the circle. The side stitches are half stitches and the 3 corner stitches are full stitches.

This is the last time you will need to begin with a standing stitch and you do so around the middle stitch of any 5-stitch corner.

## Round 8 and 9

There is nothing tricky in the last rounds. The only thing that may be a little different is the last small stitch round, as there are (2 stitches, chain 2, 2 stitches) in each corner chain space.

## Now...

After you've made your first square, weave in your ends, block it and then make notes in the project planner. Record:

- Yarn and hook used
- Size
- Weight

Once you've done all of that, make another one or more. If you used the video, try to make it using the chart or written pattern this time. Note down how many more you make as you go.

Well done! Time to move on to the next lesson.

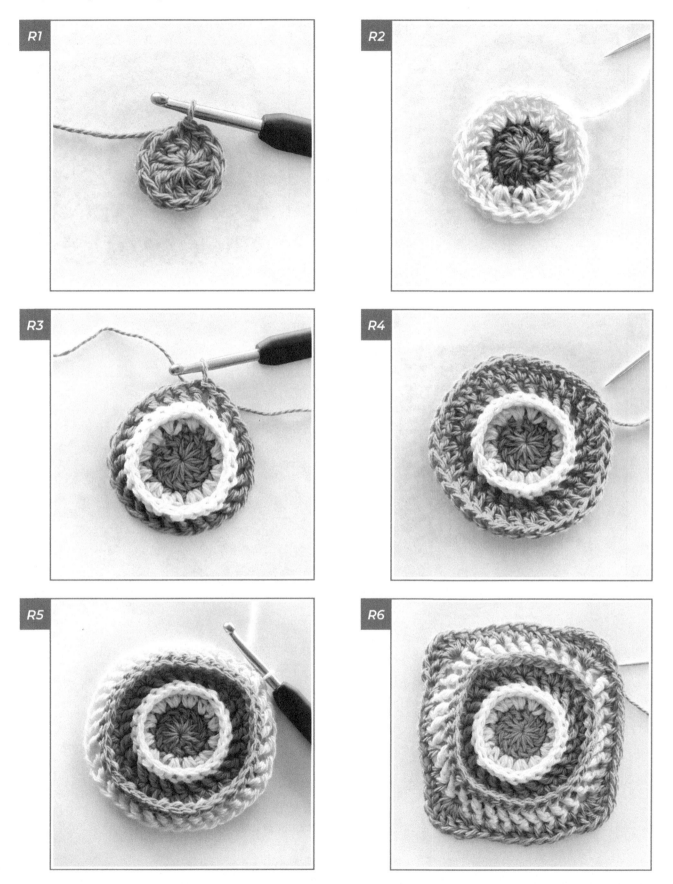

R7

R8

R9

# Part Five

## Reading

## Patterns

## Turning Terry Pattern Help

## Turning crochet

Turning crochet is most commonly done with crochet patterns worked in rows. It is rarer in granny squares.

I have designed some rows patterns, even though granny squares are my thing.

*This Charming Boy rows pattern*

For me, crochet has a very definite front and back. I design 99.9% of my patterns with the front side as the focus. Sure, some simple patterns work fine turning, but generally, the pattern I want you to see is on the front.

The reason is the front of crochet stitches look very different to the back, as we found out in the first Granny Square Academy.

Turning granny squares is often touted as the solution to correct the swirl you can get with some patterns – especially the traditional granny square.

I don't do it though unless the pattern was designed for it like the Turning Terry pattern for this lesson. To me, it makes the crochet look messy in simple patterns. And in more complex patterns, it simply won't work.

Have a close look at the basic solid granny square samples I have made.

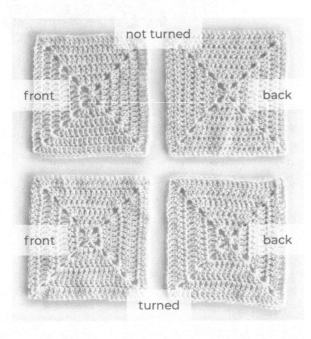

Everyone sees a different level of detail, so perhaps for you, the turned and not turned squares all look much the same. If that's the case, turning for you may be a solution for a simple pattern if your square develops a swirl.

However, there are times when turning in a granny square pattern works well and better than not turning, as is the case with the Turning Terry pattern you will make for this part.

Here is the Turning Terry pattern as written for turning, compared to the sample I made without turning.

Can you see the swirl in the not turned one? Turning has alleviated that swirl.

But why does the swirl happen? Well, think about your anatomy of a stitch again. Stitches are not symmetrical. You are usually working in the hole on the right of a stitch (left for left-handers). You can see that the swirly square pulls the stitches the right on each side. That's because I was working to the right of the stitches.

> **NOTE**
>
> **The swirl does not happen for all granny square patterns. Sometimes, a pattern may skip the first stitch of the side as a way to alleviate the swirl.**

The reason the Turning Terry pattern works being turned, and is still visually appealing, is because I have used smaller stitches for the rounds that will be on made on the wrong side, as the front and back of them is pleasing to me.

## How to read your stitches when turning

Turning crochet in granny squares does come with its challenges. If you're used to working on one side of granny squares, you're familiar with working into the hole on the right of the stitch (on the left for left-handers).

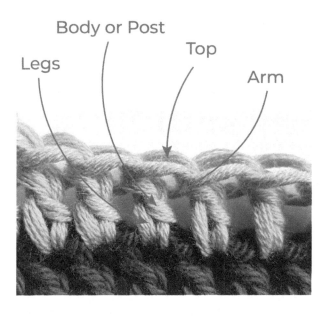

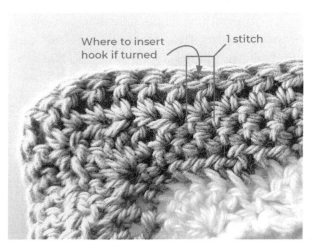

Where to insert hook if turned
1 stitch

When you turn your work, it's the opposite and it can be tricky to find the right place to work your stitches. Plus, add in working over joining stitches and it can all become very hard to read. This is why stitch markers and scraps of yarn can be very helpful.

Put a stitch marker in the last stitch of your round, as that becomes the first stitch to work into after turning and starting your corner – the blue stitch marker.

It may also pay to put a marker in the first stitch of the round as that becomes the last stitch to work into to make sure you keep on track – the red stitch marker.

Before I explain the yellow scrap of yarn, let's explore how to deal with joining with a stitch and starting the next round.

You would be used to working a stitch over your joining stitch by now. But let's think about that when we are turning.

The red needle is still under the joining stitch, which is why the next round's instructions begin with "...dc over 1-ch...". You ended the last round with chain 1 and joined with a stitch. So that chain 1 is the thing you work your first stitch over.

If you were not turning the square, you would work your first stitch of the next round, over the joining stitch, where the red needle is inserted. But have a look where the red needle is after the square is turned.

Can you see that where the red needle is, will be where you will work your last corner stitch of the next round, while the silver one is where you will work your first corner stitch?

That is the reason I recommend placing a scrap of yarn in the gap before you join a round to be turned until you become used to reading the back of your work as well as the front. It will show you clearly where to work your first and last stitches of the next round.

## New abbreviations

Turning your work brings the need for some new abbreviations. Especially with turned granny squares. They most often will have a definite right and wrong side, and the pattern instructions should tell you which side you are working on.

You will find these abbreviations in our pattern;

**RS = Right Side**

**WS = Wrong Side**

# Working rows tricks

Yes, this book is all about granny squares, but this is a good point to mention a couple of tricks if you are working rows and having troubles. Common issues are:

- Not being sure where to work your second and last stitches,
- a gap between your first and second stitches,
- and the edges not being straight.

*Left side ch3 start, right side false stitch*

As you can see, using a false stitch instead of a starting chain eliminates some of the gap, but we can do better.

## Remove the gap

After turning, slip stitch into the last stitch of the previous row and then make your starting chain or false stitch.

It's a really small thing, but as you know by now, small things can have a big impact. What working a slip stitch into the last stitch does is move where your yarn emerges from the very edge to the top of the last stitch. Then you can make your starting chain or false stitch.

Doing this also makes it really clear where to work your second stitch. If you don't do the slip stitch, it can lead to an extra stitch being added as it looks like the second stitch is the first one.

*Left side ch3 start, right side false stitch*

My last tip for making sure you keep straight edges when working in rows, is to pop a stitch marker in the 3rd chain of your starting chain or your false stitch as soon as you make it. This marks what will be the last stitch of the next row to work into. It takes out the guess work, wondering if you have worked the last stitch or not, and will therefore keep you on the straight-edged path.

# Turning Terry

## Part Five · UK Pattern

## Abbreviations

| | |
|---|---|
| cnr | corner |
| R | Round |
| rep | repeat |
| sp/s | space/s |
| st/s | stitch/es |
| stch | starting chain |
| • ss | slip stitch |
| o ch | chain |
| + dc | double crochet |
| T htr | half treble crochet |
| T tr | treble crochet |
| [RS] | right side |
| [WS] | wrong side |

Begin with mc.

R1: **[RS]** ch3 (stch), 11tr, join with ss to 3rd ch of stch.
{12 sts}

R2: **[RS]** ch3 (stch), tr in same st as ss, *tr in next 2 sts**, (2tr, ch2, 2tr) in next st*, rep from * to * 2x and * to ** 1x, 2tr in same st as first sts, ch1, join with dc to 3rd ch of stch.
{6 sts on each side; 4 2-ch cnr sps}

R3: **[WS]** turn, dc over 1-ch, *dc in next 6 sts**, (dc, ch2, dc) in 2-ch cnr sp*, rep from * to * 2x and * to ** 1x, dc in same sp as first st, ch1, join with dc to first st.
{8 sts on each side; 4 2-ch cnr sps}

R4: **[RS]** turn, dc over 1-ch, *dc in next 8 sts**, (dc, ch2, dc) in 2-ch cnr sp*, rep from * to * 2x and * to ** 1x, dc in same sp as first st, ch1, join with dc to first st.
{10 sts on each side; 4 2-ch cnr sps}

R5: **[WS]** turn, ch2 (stch), htr over 1-ch, *htr in next 10 sts**, 3htr in 2-ch cnr sp*, rep from * to * 2x and * to ** 1x, htr in same sp as first sts*, join with ss to 2nd ch of stch.
{10 sts on each side; 4 3-st cnrs}

R6: **[RS]** turn, dc in same st as ss, *dc in next 12 sts**, (dc, ch2, dc) in next st*, rep from * to * 2x and * to ** 1x, dc in same st as first st, ch1, join with dc to first st.
{14 sts on each side; 4 2-ch cnr sps}

R7: **[RS]** ch3 (stch), tr over joining dc, *7x [skip 1 st, tr in next st, tr in skipped st]**, 3tr in 2-ch cnr sp*, rep from * to * 2x and * to ** 1x, tr in same sp as first sts, join with ss to 3rd ch of stch.
{14 sts on each side; 4 3-st cnrs}

R8: **[WS]** turn, ch2 (stch), htr in same st as ss, *htr in next 16 sts**, (2htr, ch2, 2htr) in next st*, rep from * to * 2x and * to ** 1x, 2htr in same st as first sts, ch2, join with ss to 2nd ch of stch. Fasten off.
{20 sts on each side; 4 2-ch cnr sps}

## Turning Terry

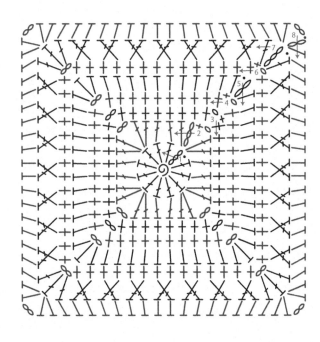

### Abbreviations

| | | |
|---|---|---|
| | cnr | corner |
| | R | Round |
| | rep | repeat |
| | sp/s | space/s |
| | st/s | stitch/es |
| | stch | starting chain |
| • | ss | slip stitch |
| ○ | ch | chain |
| + | sc | single crochet |
| T | hdc | half double crochet |
| T | dc | double crochet |
| **[RS]** | | right side |
| **[WS]** | | wrong side |

Begin with mc.

**R1:** [RS] ch3 (stch), 11dc, join with ss to 3rd ch of stch.
{12 sts}

**R2:** [RS] ch3 (stch), dc in same st as ss, *dc in next 2 sts**, (2dc, ch2, 2dc) in next st*, rep from * to * 2x and * to ** 1x, 2dc in same st as first sts, ch1, join with sc to 3rd ch of stch.
{6 sts on each side; 4 2-ch cnr sps}

**R3:** [WS] turn, sc over 1-ch, *sc in next 6 sts**, (sc, ch2, sc) in 2-ch cnr sp*, rep from * to * 2x and * to ** 1x, sc in same sp as first st, ch1, join with sc to first st.
{8 sts on each side; 4 2-ch cnr sps}

**R4:** [RS] turn, sc over 1-ch, *sc in next 8 sts**, (sc, ch2, sc) in 2-ch cnr sp*, rep from * to * 2x and * to ** 1x, sc in same sp as first st, ch1, join with sc to first st.
{10 sts on each side; 4 2-ch cnr sps}

**R5:** [WS] turn, ch2 (stch), hdc over 1-ch, *hdc in next 10 sts**, 3hdc in 2-ch cnr sp*, rep from * to * 2x and * to ** 1x, hdc in same sp as first sts*, join with ss to 2nd ch of stch.
{10 sts on each side; 4 3-st cnrs}

**R6:** [RS] turn, sc in same st as ss, *sc in next 12 sts**, (sc, ch2, sc) in next st*, rep from * to * 2x and * to ** 1x, sc in same st as first st, ch1, join with sc to first st.
{14 sts on each side; 4 2-ch cnr sps}

**R7:** [RS] ch3 (stch), dc over joining sc, *7x [skip 1 st, dc in next st, dc in skipped st]**, 3dc in 2-ch cnr sp*, rep from * to * 2x and * to ** 1x, dc in same sp as first sts, join with ss to 3rd ch of stch.
{14 sts on each side; 4 3-st cnrs}

**R8:** [WS] turn, ch2 (stch), hdc in same st as ss, *hdc in next 16 sts**, (2hdc, ch2, 2hdc) in next st*, rep from * to * 2x and * to ** 1x, 2hdc in same st as first sts, ch2, join with ss to 2nd ch of stch. Fasten off.
{20 sts on each side; 4 2-ch cnr sps}

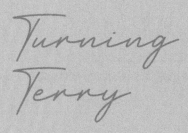

*Turning Terry*

## Pattern Help

To maximize your learning, use these notes and photos to work from as you make the pattern.

If you get stuck, watch me make the pattern in the video:

 *Turning Terry video*

 *Mirrored Turning Terry video*

Prior knowledge needed from Granny Square Academy:

▷ *Anatomy of a stitch* **Part 1**

▷ *Skipping stitches* **Part 2**

# Round 3

This is the first round where you will turn your work. That's why you will see **[WS]** at the start of the round. As it's a small stitch round, it will really help to use a stitch marker in the first stitch as soon as you make it.

After you have worked your first stitch over the 1-chain space, identify the place you will work your first stitch into the side. It may help to turn your work to the right side and insert a stitch marker or needle to show where exactly to work.

It can also be tricky to know when you have reached the end of the side. My tip is to count to 6 as you work your side stitches, and turn your work to the right side if you're not sure if you have worked the last stitch.

At the end of the round, pop a scrap of yarn into the gap before you join to help with the placement of your Round 4 stitches. Leave your stitch marker in the first stitch and place one in the last stitch if you need help in the next round.

## Round 4

Keep the stitch markers in the first and last stitches of Round 3 as you work this round, as they will show you where to work your first and last side stitches. The scrap of yarn shows you where to work the last corner stitch.

## Rounds 5 and 6

Keep using your stitch markers in the first and last stitches as well as your scrap of yarn in the gap before you join.

## Round 7

This round is much the same as a round in the Part 3 Between Billie pattern. You are making crosses by skipping a stitch, working a stitch in the next one, then working a stitch in the one you skipped. The difference is the first stitch to skip may be obscured a little by your corner stitches. If that is the case, pull them to the side to make it clear which stitch to skip.

## Now...

After you've made your first square, weave in your ends, block it and then make notes in the project planner. Record:

- Yarn and hook used
- Size
- Weight

Once you've done all of that, make another one or more. If you used the video, try to make it using the chart or written pattern this time. Note down how many more you make as you go.

Well done! Time to move on to the next lesson.

R1

R2

R3

[WS]

R4

R5

[WS]

R6

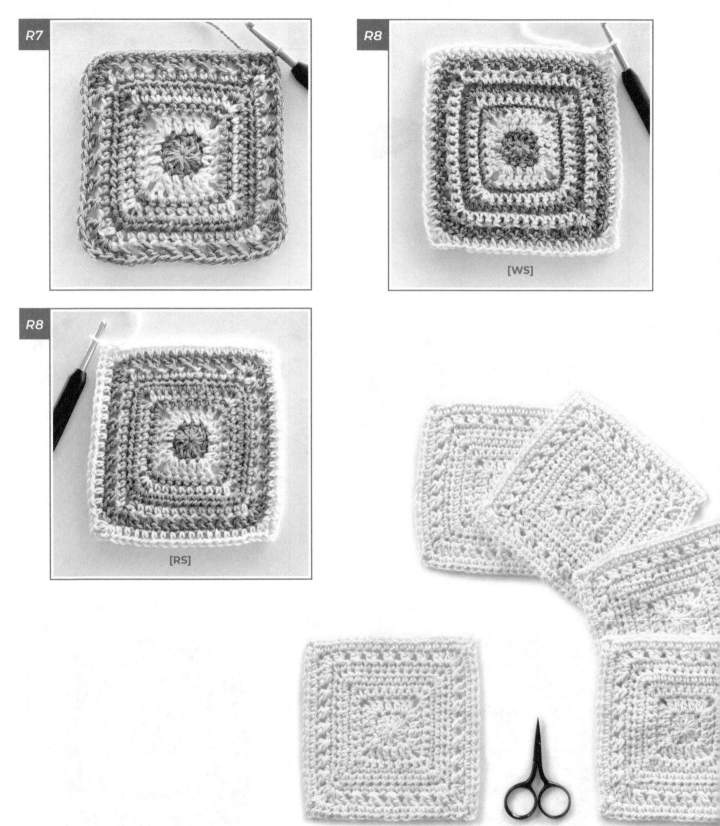

R7

R8

[WS]

R8

[RS]

# Part Six

## Reading

## Patterns

## Same Same Sam Pattern Help

## *Using the same stitch more than once*

With simple crochet, every stitch is used once. But, I am sure you have used the same stitch many times in your crochet adventures. It's very common to work more than one stitch into a stitch. The Circle Cindy pattern from the first Granny Square Academy used this technique to make the circle part.

Adding more than one stitch in any given stitch, increases the number of stitches in a round, hence it being called an increase in patterns for amigurumi.

But there is more to using the same stitch than increasing. Cool effects can be achieved by using the same stitch more than once in the same round or even in different rounds.

My Mayan pattern uses different parts of stitches more than once in the same and different rounds to create increases, surface texture and patterns.

Let's recall all the different ways we have touched on to use a stitch so far:

- in
- around as front post or back post
- in the back loop only
- in the loop behind v
- between

Now, think about all those different places you can use. You can use more than one place to work stitches. And that's what the pattern in this part is all about. Using the same stitch more than once, but in different ways.

We will be using both in and around stitches for this part. We will explore more uses of this technique in later parts.

There are a few ways to express how to use the same stitch more than once and it depends on the pattern how it is stated.

This is Round 3 of the Same Same Sam UK terms pattern, expressed in different ways.

R3: ch3 (stch), (tr in, fptr around) next st, *tr in next st, (tr in, fptr around) next st*, rep from * to * 10x, join with ss to 3rd ch of stch.

## OR

R3: ch3 (stch), tr in next st, fptr around same st as last st, *tr in next 2 sts, fptr around same st as last st*, rep from * to * 10x, join with ss to 3rd ch of stch.

Both of these sets of instructions for Round 3 will give the same result. Most commonly, the briefer way is used:

> *"...(tr in, fptr around) next st, ..."*

Remember from your reading pattern instructions in Part 1 of the first Granny Square Academy that one instruction is contained between commas. What you see above is one instruction.

It means that you are to work the contents of the brackets using the next stitch in different ways. 1 stitch in the next stitch and a front post stitch around the same stitch.

In the circle, every stitch has been used twice, once in and once around.

The order and contents of those brackets can be different:

*"... (fptr around, tr in) next st, ..."*

*or*

*"... (fptr around, tr in, fptr around) next st, ..."*

...which is shown as the corner in this photo.

Now let's look at another way to express how to use the same stitch that is needed sometimes:

*"... tr in next st, fptr around same st as last st, ..."*

This has separated the instruction into two parts. The instruction to use the same stitch is left until the second part, where you work a front post around the same stitch as the last stitch. We learned what "last stitch" means in Part 3.

## Tip for using the same stitch

If you need to work a stitch into a stitch that already has a front post stitch worked around it, pull the front post stitch down the post and the "P" to work into will appear.

The red needle is pointing to where to work a stitch **in** after one has been worked **around**.

# Same Same Sam

## Part Six · UK Pattern

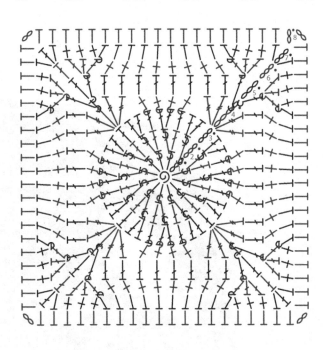

## Abbreviations

| | | |
|---|---|---|
| | cnr | corner |
| | R | Round |
| | rep | repeat |
| | sp/s | space/s |
| | st/s | stitch/es |
| | stch | starting chain |
| • | ss | slip stitch |
| o | ch | chain |
| + | dc | double crochet |
| T | htr | half treble crochet |
| ⌡ | tr | treble crochet |
| ⌡ | dtr | double treble crochet |
| ɔ | fp | front post |
| c | bp | back post |

Begin with mc.

**R1:** ch3 (stch), 11tr, join with ss to 3rd ch of stch.
{12 sts}

**R2:** ch3 (stch), fptr around same st as ss, *(tr in, fptr around) next st*, rep from * to * 10x, join with ss to 3rd ch of stch.
{24 sts}

**R3:** ch3 (stch), tr in next st, fptr around same st as last st, *tr in next 2 sts, fptr around same st as last st*, rep from * to * 10x, join with ss to 3rd ch of stch.
{36 sts}

**OR**

**R3:** ch3 (stch), (tr in, fptr around) next st, *tr in next st, (tr in, fptr around) next st*, rep from * to * 10x, join with ss to 3rd ch of stch.
{36 sts}

**R4:** ch4 (stch), 2dtr in same st as ss, *skip 2 sts, bpdc around next 4 sts, skip 2 sts**, 5dtr in next st*, rep from * to * 2x and * to ** 1x, 2dtr in same st as first sts, join with ss to 4th ch of stch.
{4 sts on each side; 4 5-st cnrs}

**R5:** ch3 (stch), fptr around same st as ss, *tr in next 8 sts**, (fptr around, tr in, fptr around) next st*, rep from * to * 2x and * to ** 1x, fptr around same st as first sts, join with ss to 3rd ch of stch.
{10 sts on each side; 4 1-st cnrs}

**R6:** ch3 (stch), *(2tr in, fptr around) next st, dc in next 8 sts, (fptr around, 2tr in) next st**, tr in next st*, rep from * to * 2x and * to ** 1x, join with ss to 3rd ch of stch.
{14 sts on each side; 4 1-st cnrs}

**R7:** ch3 (stch), htr in same st as ss, *dc in next 2 sts, (dc in, fphtr around) next st, htr in next 8 sts, (fphtr around, dc in) next st, dc in next 2 sts**, (htr, tr, htr) in next st*, rep from * to * 2x and * to ** 1x, htr in same st as first sts, join with ss to 3rd ch of stch.
{16 sts on each side; 4 3-st cnrs}

**R8:** ch2 (stch), *htr in next 18 sts**, (htr, ch2, htr) in next st*, rep from * to * 2x and * to ** 1x, htr in same st as first st, ch2, join with ss to 2nd ch of stch.
Fasten off.
{20 sts on each side; 4 2-ch cnr sps}

# Same Same Sam

## Part Six · US Pattern

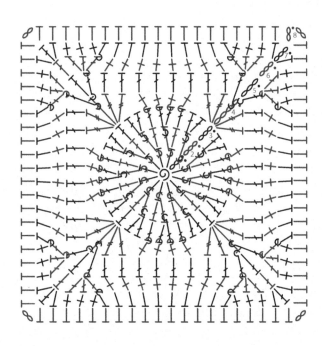

## Abbreviations

| | | |
|---|---|---|
| | cnr | corner |
| | R | Round |
| | rep | repeat |
| | sp/s | space/s |
| | st/s | stitch/es |
| | stch | starting chain |
| • | ss | slip stitch |
| ○ | ch | chain |
| + | sc | single crochet |
| ⊤ | hdc | half double crochet |
| ⊤ | dc | double crochet |
| ⊤ | tr | triple crochet |
| つ | fp | front post |
| ⊂ | bp | back post |

Begin with mc.

**R1:** ch3 (stch), 11dc, join with ss to 3rd ch of stch.
{12 sts}

**R2:** ch3 (stch), fpdc around same st as ss, *(dc in, fpdc around) next st*, rep from * to * 10x, join with ss to 3rd ch of stch.
{24 sts}

**R3:** ch3 (stch), dc in next st, fpdc around same st as last st, *dc in next 2 sts, fpdc around same st as last st*, rep from * to * 10x, join with ss to 3rd ch of stch.
{36 sts}

OR

**R3:** ch3 (stch), (dc in, fpdc around) next st, *dc in next st, (dc in, fpdc around) next st*, rep from * to * 10x, join with ss to 3rd ch of stch.
{36 sts}

**R4:** ch4 (stch), 2tr in same st as ss, *skip 2 sts, bpsc around next 4 sts, skip 2 sts**, 5tr in next st*, rep from * to * 2x and * to ** 1x, 2tr in same st as first sts, join with ss to 4th ch of stch.
{4 sts on each side; 4 5-st cnrs}

**R5:** ch3 (stch), fpdc around same st as ss, *dc in next 8 sts**, (fpdc around, dc in, fpdc around) next st*, rep from * to * 2x and * to ** 1x, fpdc around same st as first sts, join with ss to 3rd ch of stch.
{10 sts on each side; 4 1-st cnrs}

**R6:** ch3 (stch), *(2dc in, fpdc around) next st, sc in next 8 sts, (fpdc around, 2dc in) next st**, dc in next st*, rep from * to * 2x and * to ** 1x, join with ss to 3rd ch of stch.
{14 sts on each side; 4 1-st cnrs}

**R7:** ch3 (stch), hdc in same st as ss, *sc in next 2 sts, (sc in, fphdc around) next st, hdc in next 8 sts, (fphdc around, sc in) next st, sc in next 2 sts**, (hdc, dc, hdc) in next st*, rep from * to * 2x and * to ** 1x, hdc in same st as first sts, join with ss to 3rd ch of stch.
{16 sts on each side; 4 3-st cnrs}

**R8:** ch2 (stch), *hdc in next 18 sts**, (hdc, ch2, hdc) in next st*, rep from * to * 2x and * to ** 1x, hdc in same st as first st, ch2, join with ss to 2nd ch of stch. Fasten off.
{20 sts on each side; 4 2-ch cnr sps}

# Same Same Sam

## Pattern Help

To maximize your learning, use these notes and photos to work from as you make the pattern.

If you get stuck, watch me make the pattern in the video:

 *Same Same Sam video*

 *Mirrored Same Same Sam video*

Prior knowledge needed from Granny Square Academy:

▷ *Making back post stitches* **Part 5**

▷ *Making front post stitches* **Part 6**

## Round 2

The first time you will use the same stitch twice is at the very start. You will use the same stitch as slip stitch, i.e. the first stitch of Round 1 you joined into. That could be chain 3 or a false stitch.

After making your starting chain or false stitch for this round, work a front post stitch around the same stitch as the slip stitch.

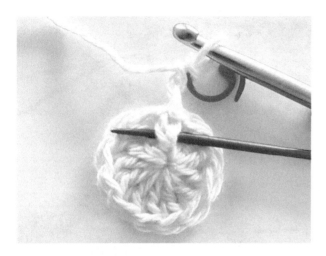

The rest of the Round 1 stitches are used twice in the same way – a stitch is worked in them and then a stitch around them.

## Round 3

Just like a flat circle, in this round we are increasing by working 2 stitches every second stitch. The difference from a flat citcle is, the second stitch using the same stitch is a front post stitch. The front posts should always be around the front post stitches of Round 2.

## Round 5

The corners are where you will use 1 stitch more than once. This time, you will use the middle stitch of the 5-stitch corners three times.

At the start, you will work 1 front post stitch after your starting chain or false stitch around the same stitch as slip stitch. You will work the third stitch of that first corner at the end.

The next 3 corners you will use the middle stitch of the 5 corner stitches three times. First, a front post around it. Pull it down if you have trouble seeing where to work the next stitch into the same stitch.

Then you work another front post around the same stitch.

The last stitch of the round is a front post around the same stitch you worked a front post around at the start.

## Round 6

Once again, at times along the side, you will be using the same stitch to work into and around. The front post stitches are always worked around the front post stitches of Round 5.

## Now...

After you've made your first square, weave in your ends, block it and then make notes in the project planner. Record:

- Yarn and hook used
- Size
- Weight

Once you've done all of that, make another one or more. If you used the video, try to make it using the chart or written pattern this time. Note down how many more you make as you go.

Well done! Time to move on to the next lesson.

R1

R2

R3

R4

R5

R6

R7

R8

# Part Seven

## Reading

## Patterns

## Popcorn Perry Pattern Help

## *Traditional popcorns*

I love the texture and shape of popcorn stitches. I use them quite often, but I find the traditional way to make them annoying.

Popcorn stitches are made by working a set of stitches, then you take your hook out and slip stitch the first stitch to the last. It messes with your flow.

*Make 5 stitches, remove hook and insert into first stitch*

*Grab working loop and slip stitch to form popcorn*

# Lazy popcorns

I came up with a way to make poporn stitches I call the lazy way. This is not a technique you can swap for any pattern that uses popcorns. The pattern needs to have been designed with lazy popcorns as it takes two rounds to make them.

I don't call them popcorns in the pattern instructions because they take two rounds to create.

In the first lazy popcorn round, I make sets of stitches, usually with a 1-chain space on either side.

It can make for some crazy looking, super wavy crochet! This is where you need to trust the pattern. In the second lazy popcorn round, the magic happens. You gather each set of 5 stitches together by making 1 stitch in both chain spaces either side of the 5 stitches at once. You poke your hook under the 5 stitches to make your gathering stitch.

This photo was taken part way through the second round of making lazy popcorns in my Nimue pattern.

The Popcorn Perry pattern I designed for this part incorporates both the traditional popcorns and my lazy ones.

**NOTE**

When making a traditional popcorn as the first stitch, it is usually known as a beginning popcorn made up of ch3 (stch) plus 4 stitches. You can do a false stitch instead of that chain 3 as discussed in Part 1. It doesn't really make much difference in a popcorn stitch, but I do it anyway.

## Traditional popcorns and lazy popcorns comparison

Another reason I like to design patterns with popcorns created the lazy way, is that they sit straighter than traditionally made popcorns as you can see here. You will likely note this difference yourself as you make the Popcorn Perry pattern.

lazy popcorn    lazy popcorn

traditional popcorn

# Working into popcorns

When working a stitch into a popcorn stitch, regardless of how the popcorn was made, there are two options. Thinking of a regular stitch, you'd usually poke your hook into the hole like the capital P. However, I like to work into the middle of the popcorn.

How do you know which one to do? Well, if I say "in the next st", that is how you would normally work into a stitch. If I say "in the top of the pc", that means you poke your hook in the middle of the popcorn instead. Squish your popcorn stitch a little and you will see the hole in the middle of the popcorn stitch.

*in popcorn*

*in top of popcorn*

## NOTE

Popcorns are usually made up of 5 regular stitches, but they can be other types of stitches and a different number as well. For example, you could have a popcorn made by making 6 dtr/tr (UK/US) stitches. The abbreviations list for your pattern should tell you what type and how many stitches you need to make for your popcorn if it varies from the standard 5 tr/dc (UK/US).

# Layered front post stitches

While this part is all about popcorns, there is a phenomenon I want to tell you about with regards to front post stitches.

In the first granny Square Academy when you learned about front post stitches, you heard about the way front post stitches can cause a dip along your sides. That is when just one or a few stitches in a round are worked as front posts.

When you work most stitches in more than one round as a front post stitch, a strange thing happens.

You will find your work curling up or cupping. Normally if this happens, it means that there are not enough stitches and so your work cups.

However, when you work only front post stitches, that's not the case. It is more like Tunisian crochet in the way the fabric behaves. It curls up, but once you block it, the work will sit perfectly flat. The reason it happens is you are working on top of the previous round entirely. Think of the front posts as being laid on top of the previous round.

Tunisian crochet

# Popcorn Perry

## Part Seven · UK Pattern

## Abbreviations

| | | |
|---|---|---|
| | cnr | corner |
| | R | Round |
| | rep | repeat |
| | sp/s | space/s |
| | st/s | stitch/es |
| | stch | starting chain |
| • | ss | slip stitch |
| ∘ | ch | chain |
| + | dc | double crochet |
| T | htr | half treble crochet |
| T | tr | treble crochet |
| ∮ | hdtr | half double treble crochet |
| ∮ | dtr | double treble crochet |
| ⊕ | pc | popcorn (5tr) |
| ↄ | fp | front post |
| (⟋‾⟍) | | at the same time |

**Begin with mc.**

R1: ch3 (stch), 15tr, join with ss to 3rd ch of stch.
{16 sts}

R2: ch3 (stch), *pc in next st**, 2tr in next st*, rep from * to * 6x and * to ** 1x, tr in same st as first st, join with ss to 3rd ch of stch.
{24 sts}

R3: 2dc in same st as ss, *dc in top of pc**, 2dc in next 2 sts*, rep from * to * 6x and * to ** 1x, 2dc in next st, join with ss to first st.
{40 sts}

**R4 will be very ruffled.**

R4: ch3 (stch), tr in next st, *ch1, 5tr in next st, ch1**, tr in next 4 sts*, rep from * to * 6x and * to ** 1x, tr in next 2 sts, join with ss to 3rd ch of stch.
{72 sts, 16 1-ch sps}

R5: dc in same st as ss, dc in next st, *dc in in both 1-ch sps either side of next 5 sts at the same time**, dc in next 4 sts*, rep from * to * 6x and * to ** 1x, dc in next 2 sts, join with ss to first st.
{40 sts}

R6: ch4 (stch), hdtr in same st as ss, *tr in next 2 sts, htr in next 2 sts, dc in next st, htr in next 2 sts, tr in next 2 sts**, (hdtr, dtr, ch2, dtr, hdtr) in next st*, rep from * to * 2x and * to ** 1x, (hdtr, dtr) in same st as first sts, ch1, join with dc to 4th ch of stch.
{13 sts on each side; 4 2-ch cnr sps}

R7: ch3 (stch), htr over joining dc, *fptr around next 13 sts**, (htr, tr, htr) in 2-ch cnr sp*, rep from * to * 2x and * to ** 1x, htr in same sp as first sts, join with ss to 3rd ch of stch.
{13 sts on each side; 4 3-st cnrs}

R8: ch3 (stch), htr in same st as ss, *fptr around next 15 sts**, (htr, tr, htr) in next st*, rep from * to * 2x and * to ** 1x, htr in same st as first sts, join with ss to 3rd ch of stch.
{15 sts on each side; 4 3-st cnrs}

R9: dc in same st as ss, *dc in next 17 sts**, (dc, ch2, dc) in next st*, rep from * to * 2x and * to ** 1x, dc in same st as first st, ch2, join with ss to first st.
Fasten off.
{19 sts on each side; 4 2-ch cnr sps}

# Popcorn Perry

## Part Seven · US Pattern

## Abbreviations

| | | |
|---|---|---|
| | cnr | corner |
| | R | Round |
| | rep | repeat |
| | sp/s | space/s |
| | st/s | stitch/es |
| | stch | starting chain |
| • | ss | slip stitch |
| o | ch | chain |
| + | sc | single crochet |
| T | hdc | half double crochet |
| T | dc | double crochet |
| T | htr | half triple crochet |
| T | tr | triple crochet |
| ⊕ | pc | popcorn (5dc) |
| ↺ | fp | front post |
| ⬭ | | at the same time |

Begin with mc.

R1: ch3 (stch), 15dc, join with ss to 3rd ch of stch.
{16 sts}

R2: ch3 (stch), *pc in next st**, 2dc in next st*, rep from * to * 6x and * to ** 1x, dc in same st as first st, join with ss to 3rd ch of stch.
{24 sts}

R3: 2sc in same st as ss, *sc in top of pc**, 2sc in next 2 sts*, rep from * to * 6x and * to ** 1x, 2sc in next st, join with ss to first st.
{40 sts}

**R4 will be very ruffled.**

R4: ch3 (stch), dc in next st, *ch1, 5dc in next st, ch1**, dc in next 4 sts*, rep from * to * 6x and * to ** 1x, dc in next 2 sts, join with ss to 3rd ch of stch.
{72 sts, 16 1-ch sps}

R5: sc in same st as ss, sc in next st, *sc in in both 1-ch sps either side of next 5 sts at the same time**, sc in next 4 sts*, rep from * to * 6x and * to ** 1x, sc in next 2 sts, join with ss to first st.
{40 sts}

R6: ch4 (stch), htr in same st as ss, *dc in next 2 sts, hdc in next 2 sts, sc in next st, hdc in next 2 sts, dc in next 2 sts**, (htr, tr, ch2, tr, htr) in next st*, rep from * to * 2x and * to ** 1x, (htr, tr) in same st as first sts, ch1, join with sc to 4th ch of stch.
{13 sts on each side; 4 2-ch cnr sps}

R7: ch3 (stch), hdc over joining sc, *fpdc around next 13 sts**, (hdc, dc, hdc) in 2-ch cnr sp*, rep from * to * 2x and * to ** 1x, hdc in same sp as first sts, join with ss to 3rd ch of stch.
{13 sts on each side; 4 3-st cnrs}

R8: ch3 (stch), hdc in same st as ss, *fpdc around next 15 sts**, (hdc, dc, hdc) in next st*, rep from * to * 2x and * to ** 1x, hdc in same st as first sts, join with ss to 3rd ch of stch.
{15 sts on each side; 4 3-st cnrs}

R9: sc in same st as ss, *sc in next 17 sts**, (sc, ch2, sc) in next st*, rep from * to * 2x and * to ** 1x, sc in same st as first st, ch2, join with ss to first st. Fasten off.
{19 sts on each side; 4 2-ch cnr sps}

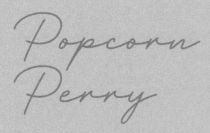

# Popcorn Perry

## Pattern Help

To maximize your learning, use these notes and photos to work from as you make the pattern.

If you get stuck, watch me make the pattern in the video:

 *Popcorn Perry video*

 *Mirrored Popcorn Perry video*

Prior knowledge needed from Granny Square Academy:

▷ *Front posts*
**Part 6**

▷ *Circle to Square*
**Part 7**

## Round 2

You'll be making traditional popcorns in this round.

Between each popcorn there are 2 regular stitches in 1 stitch.

## Round 3

A simple round with just small stitches, the only thing that may be new to you is where to work the stitch into the popcorn stitch. If you have trouble finding the middle of the popcorn, give it a gentle squeeze and you should see the hole open up.

## Round 4

This is the first of our two lazy popcorn rounds. The 5 stitches in one should fall in the stitch in the popcorns. Remember to chain 1 either side of your 5 stitches. The 4 stitches either side of the the lazy popcorns have a single stitch worked into each of them.

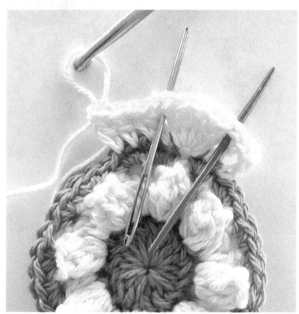

This round will be very wavy! Trust the pattern.

## Round 5

Now the magic happens! After your first 2 stitches of the side, you will finish your first lazy popcorn. Insert your hook under the 5 stitches and make your single small stitch.

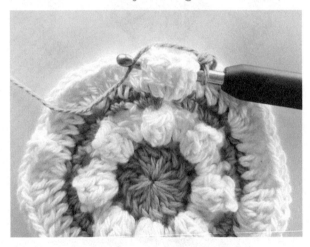

## Round 9

You will find your Popcorn Perry lifting up along the sides. Blocking will fix it.

## Now...

After you've made your first square, weave in your ends, block it and then make notes in the project planner. Record:

- Yarn and hook used
- Size
- Weight

Once you've done all of that, make another one or more. If you used the video, try to make it using the chart or written pattern this time. Note down how many more you make as you go.

Well done! Time to move on to the next lesson.

*Round by round photos of Popcorn Perry*

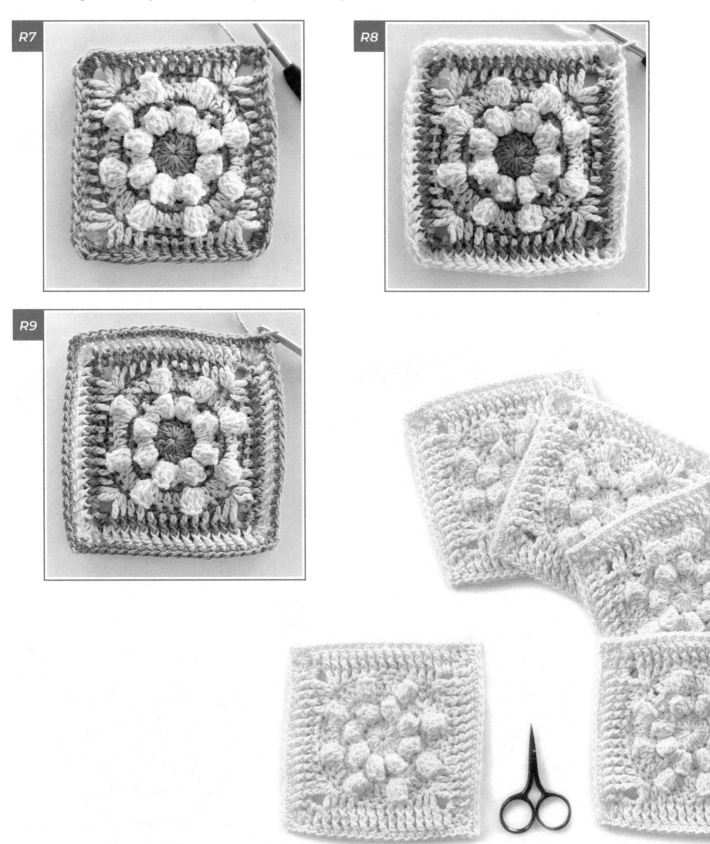

# Part Eight

## Reading

## Patterns

## Other Round Ricky Pattern Help

## Working into different rounds

Most often when making granny squares, you use the stitches of the previous round to work into, around or skip. It's a given that you are using the previous round, so it is not necessary to specify what round to work into.

In more complex, textured granny squares that texture is often achieved by using a stitch or chain space of an earlier round than the previous round. And sometimes more than one earlier round as well as the previous round is used.

*Bellinghausen*

This is when a pattern will specify a round or rounds to work certain or all stitches. Take this excerpt from my Bellinghausen pattern from Granny Square Flair and Siren's Atlas:

R8: ...*tr in next st, tr in next 5 sts of R6 behind R7 sts, htr in next 5 sts, tr in next 5 sts of R6 behind R7 sts, tr in next st*...

You'll note some instructions specify what round you need to work into or skip, and some don't.

If it doesn't say a specific round, you use the just completed round.

The reason every instruction doesn't specify a round is for brevity's sake. It's a crochet norm not to say what round to work into unless needed. If patterns stated what round every stitch was to be made into, they would be much longer than they needed to be. The more words there are, the harder a pattern is to follow and keep track of. I only specify another round if the one you need to use is not the previous round.

## How do you use other rounds?

As you have learned in previous parts, there are many ways a stitch can be used. For example, working a front or back post stitch, you work around the post of the stitch only. This leaves the top of the stitch, the "v" you'd usually use free to be used. We used both around the post and in the same stitch in Part 6.

Well, the same principle applies when using stitches or chain spaces from rounds other than the last one worked. That's where you'll see a bit more in the instruction. It is possible to work behind other stitches, in front of them or over them so you will see extra words like:

- behind R7 sts,
- in front of R3 & R4,
- over 2-ch space into R6 st below
- in skipped stitch of R8 in front of R7

The red needle in the following photos demonstrates where to insert your hook if you need to work behind, in front or over stitches or chain spaces.

## Working behind

When working behind either chain spaces or stitches of previous rounds, it may help to fold the front stitches down to make the stitches behind easier to see.

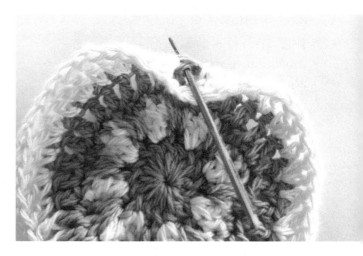

## Working in front

When working in front, it may help to fold the stitches behind the stitches or chain spaces back so you don't catch them as you work your stitches in front.

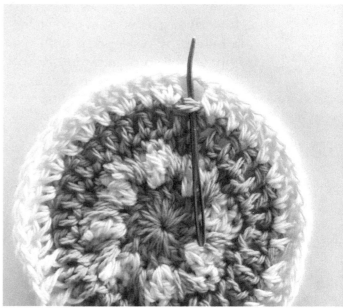

## Working over

When working over a chain space into a previous round, you encase the chain space in the stitch you are making. We will cover working over a stitch in a later part.

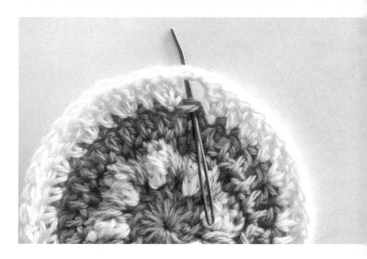

Let's look at the technique with an actual pattern and break it down.

This is the first three rounds from the Illudium pattern in Granny Square Patchwork:

R1:  ch3 (stch), 15tr, join with ss to 3rd ch of stch.
{16 sts}

R2:  ch3 (stch), tr in same st as ss, *ch2, skip 1 st**, 2tr in next st*, rep from * to * 6x and * to ** 1x, join with ss to 3rd ch of stch.
{16 sts, 8 2-ch sps}

R3:  dc in same st as ss, dc in next st, *dc in 2-ch sp, pc in skipped st of R1 in front of 2-ch sp, dc in same 2-ch sp**, dc in next 2 sts*, rep from * to * 6x and * to ** 1x, join with ss to first st.
{40 sts}

In the first round, there are 16 stitches. In the second round, every second stitch of Round 1 is skipped. In the third round, you use the skipped stitch of Round 1, as well as the stitches and chain spaces of Round 2. The red needle shows where you insert your hook and work the popcorn in front of the chain space.

TIP

**It can be confusing with the extra words and instructions. Take your time. Remember to work from comma to comma, one instruction at a time.**

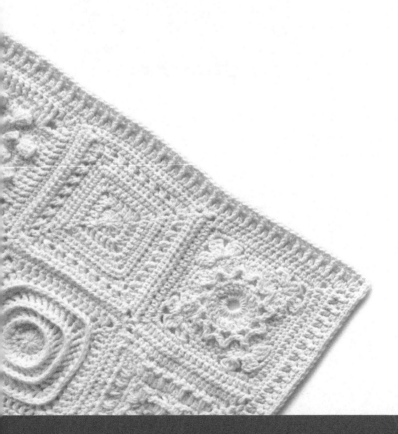

# Textured, layered crochet charts

If you are a chart user rather than a written pattern user, things can get tricky to read with textured, layered granny squares. Charts are flat, two-dimensional representations of a crochet pattern. It is really hard to clearly show when stitches are worked in front of or behind other rounds of stitches.

This is a snippet of a chart for the start of the Piazza pattern from Granny Square Patchwork.

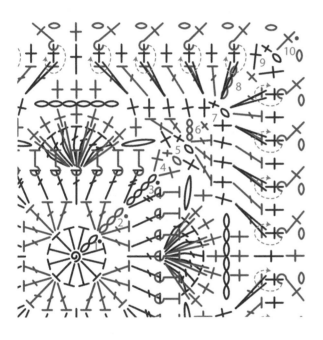

More than one round is used a lot in this pattern. I think you will agree it's a bit hard to read!

This is the one side and one corner repeat for Round 5 of the pattern:

*ch1, 7tr in 4th st of R3 behind R4 sts, ch1**, (dc,ch2, dc) in 2-ch cnr sp*

Taking the time to read the written pattern should help you make sense of the chart.

In the charts you will see for the Other Round Ricky pattern, you may note that some symbols have a curve in the stitch symbol. This is an indication that the stitch is to be worked in front or behind the previous round/s.

A left bend indicates behind and a right bend, in front.

behind          in front

But still, the charts for layered crochet patterns are harder to read no matter how they are shown, so remember to refer to the written pattern if you are having trouble interpreting a chart.

# Other Round Ricky

## Part Eight · UK Pattern

## Abbreviations

| | | |
|---|---|---|
| | cnr | corner |
| | R | Round |
| | rep | repeat |
| | sp/s | space/s |
| | st/s | stitch/es |
| | stch | starting chain |
| • | ss | slip stitch |
| o | ch | chain |
| + | dc | double crochet |
| T | htr | half treble crochet |
| 十 | tr | treble crochet |
| 十 | dtr | double treble crochet |
| ᒐ | fp | front post |
| ⬦ | cl | cluster |

Begin with mc.

*R1:* ch3 (stch), 2tr, *ch2, 3tr*, rep from * to * 2x, ch1, join with dc to 3rd ch of stch.
{3 sts on each side; 4 2-ch cnr sps}

*R2:* ch3 (stch), htr over joining dc, *fptr around next 3 sts**, (htr, tr, htr) in 2-ch cnr sp*, rep from * to * 2x and * to ** 1x, htr in same sp as first sts, join with ss to 3rd ch of stch.
{3 sts in each side; 4 3-st cnrs}

*R3:* dc in same st as ss, *dc in next st, tr in next 3 sts of R1 behind R2 sts, skip 3 sts, dc in next st**, (dc, ch2, dc) in next st*, rep from * to * 2x and * to ** 1x, dc in same st as first st, ch1, join with dc to first st.
{7 sts on each side; 4 2-ch cnr sps}

*R4:* ch3 (stch), *tr in next 7 sts**, (tr, ch2, tr) in 2-ch cnr sp*, rep from * to * 2x and * to ** 1x, tr in same sp as first st, ch1, join with dc to 3rd ch of stch.
{9 sts on each side; 4 2-ch cnr sps}

*R5:* dc over joining dc, *4x [dc in next st, ch2, skip 1 st], dc in next st**, (dc, ch2, dc) in 2-ch cnr sp*, rep from * to * 2x and * to ** 1x, dc in same sp as first st, ch1, join with dc to first st.
{7 sts, 4 2-ch sps on each side; 4 2-ch cnr sps}

*R6:* ch3 (stch), *tr in next 2 sts, 4x [dtr in skipped st of R4 behind R5 sts, skip 2-ch sp, tr in next st], tr in next st**, (tr, ch2, tr) in 2-ch cnr sp*, rep from * to * 2x and * to ** 1x, tr in same sp as first st, ch1, join with dc to 3rd ch of stch.
{13 sts on each side; 4 2-ch cnr sps}

*R7:* dc over joining dc, *dc in next 3 sts, 4x [3trcl in 2-ch sp of R5 in front of R6 sts, skip 1 st, dc in next st], dc in next 2 sts**, (dc, ch2, dc) in 2-ch cnr sp*, rep from * to * 2x and * to ** 1x, dc in same sp as first st, ch1, join with dc to first st.
{15 sts on each side; 4 2-ch cnr sps}

*R8:* ch2 (stch), *htr in next 4 sts, 4x [2tr in skipped st of R6 behind R7 sts, skip 1 st, htr in next st], htr in next 3 sts**, (htr, ch2, htr) in 2-ch cnr sp*, rep from * to * 2x and * to ** 1x, htr in same sp as first st, ch2, join with ss to 2nd ch of stch. Fasten off.
{21 sts on each side; 4 2-ch cnr sps}

# Other Round Ricky

## Part Eight · US Pattern

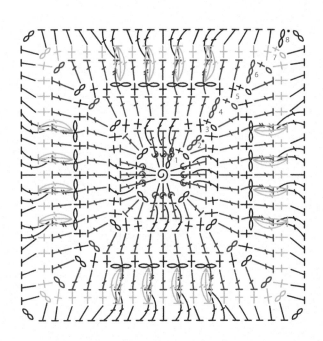

## Abbreviations

| | cnr | corner |
|---|---|---|
| | R | Round |
| | rep | repeat |
| | sp/s | space/s |
| | st/s | stitch/es |
| | stch | starting chain |
| • | ss | slip stitch |
| ○ | ch | chain |
| + | sc | single crochet |
| T | hdc | half double crochet |
| T | dc | double crochet |
| T | tr | triple crochet |
| ↄ | fp | front post |
| ⬥ | cl | cluster |

**Begin with mc.**

R1: ch3 (stch), 2dc, *ch2, 3dc*, rep from * to * 2x, ch1, join with sc to 3rd ch of stch.
{3 sts on each side; 4 2-ch cnr sps}

R2: ch3 (stch), hdc over joining sc, *fpdc around next 3 sts**, (hdc, dc, hdc) in 2-ch cnr sp*, rep from * to * 2x and * to ** 1x, hdc in same sp as first sts, join with ss to 3rd ch of stch.
{3 sts in each side; 4 3-st cnrs}

R3: sc in same st as ss, *sc in next st, dc in next 3 sts of R1 behind R2 sts, skip 3 sts, sc in next st**, (sc, ch2, sc) in next st*, rep from * to * 2x and * to ** 1x, sc in same st as first st, ch1, join with sc to first st.
{7 sts on each side; 4 2-ch cnr sps}

R4: ch3 (stch), *dc in next 7 sts**, (dc, ch2, dc) in 2-ch cnr sp*, rep from * to * 2x and * to ** 1x, dc in same sp as first st, ch1, join with sc to 3rd ch of stch.
{9 sts on each side; 4 2-ch cnr sps}

R5: sc over joining sc, *4x [sc in next st, ch2, skip 1 st], sc in next st**, (sc, ch2, sc) in 2-ch cnr sp*, rep from * to * 2x and * to ** 1x, sc in same sp as first st, ch1, join with sc to first st.
{7 sts, 4 2-ch sps on each side; 4 2-ch cnr sps}

R6: ch3 (stch), *dc in next 2 sts, 4x [tr in skipped st of R4 behind R5 sts, skip 2-ch sp, dc in next st], dc in next st**, (dc, ch2, dc) in 2-ch cnr sp*, rep from * to * 2x and * to ** 1x, dc in same sp as first st, ch1, join with sc to 3rd ch of stch.
{13 sts on each side; 4 2-ch cnr sps}

R7: sc over joining sc, *sc in next 3 sts, 4x [3dccl in 2-ch sp of R5 in front of R6 sts, skip 1 st, sc in next st], sc in next 2 sts**, (sc, ch2, sc) in 2-ch cnr sp*, rep from * to * 2x and * to ** 1x, sc in same sp as first st, ch1, join with sc to first st.
{15 sts on each side; 4 2-ch cnr sps}

R8: ch2 (stch), *hdc in next 4 sts, 4x [2dc in skipped st of R6 behind R7 sts, skip 1 st, hdc in next st], hdc in next 3 sts**, (hdc, ch2, hdc) in 2-ch cnr sp*, rep from * to * 2x and * to ** 1x, hdc in same sp as first st, ch2, join with ss to 2nd ch of stch. Fasten off.
{21 sts on each side; 4 2-ch cnr sps}

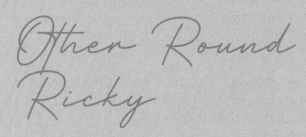

# Other Round Ricky

## Pattern Help

To maximize your learning, use these notes and photos to work from as you make the pattern.

If you get stuck, watch me make the pattern in the video:

 *Other Round Ricky video*

 *Mirrored Other Round Ricky video*

Prior knowledge needed from Granny Square Academy:

▷ *Skipping stitches*
**Part 2**

▷ *Making front post stitches*
**Part 6**

▷ *Clusters*
**Part 8**

## Round 3

This is the first time you will work behind into an earlier round. Fold your work towards you to expose the tops of the Round 1 stitches.

The 3 stitches to skip are the 3 front post stitches you made in Round 2. The last stitch of the side needs to have a stitch worked into it before you make the corner.

## Round 6

In this round you are again working behind the chain spaces of the previous round into Round 4 stitches, but you are also working into the Round 5 stitches. You alternate between Rounds 4 and 5.

## Round 7

At last you get to play with working in front! This time you will be working a cluster into the chain space of Round 5 as well as some Round 6 stitches. As you work your clusters, fold the Round 6 stitches back.

The instruction to "skip 1 st" refers to the larger stitch you worked behind the chain space in Round 6 – the red needle is showing it here and the silver needle is the next stitch to work into.

## Round 8

The last round and once more you are working behind, this time into the tall stitch made behind in Round 6. What's different is you are working 2 stitches into these behind stitches. You will skip the clusters of Round 7 and work a single stitch into the other Round 7 stitches.

Once you have finished, you may notice the centre of your square is a little swirled. As you block it, twist the centre and pin in place to correct that.

## Now...

After you've made your first square, weave in your ends, block it and then make notes in the project planner. Record:

- Yarn and hook used
- Size
- Weight

Once you've done all of that, make another one or more. If you used the video, try to make it using the chart or written pattern this time. Note down how many more you make as you go.

Well done! Time to move on to the next lesson.

R7

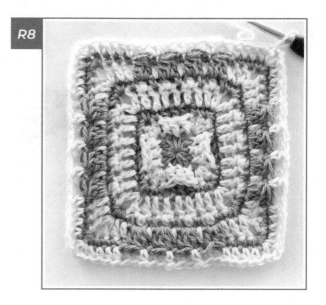

R8

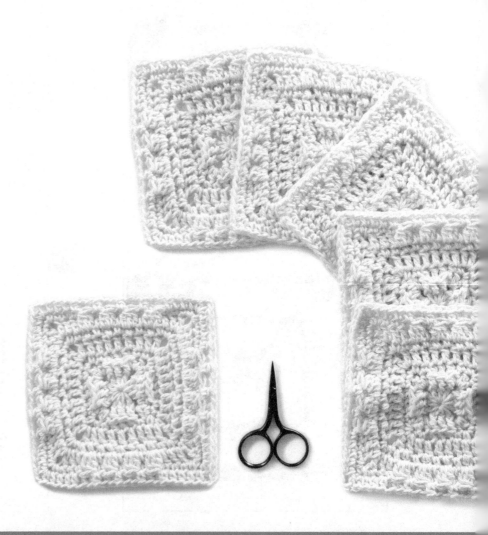

# Part Nine

## Reading

## Patterns

## Bob Leans On Flo Pattern Help

## Using the back and front loops of stitches

Most often when crocheting, you use both loops of the "v" on top of a stitch to work into.

You have used the back loop only in the first Granny Square Academy and in the Part 1 pattern of this book.

This time, I'll be teaching you how to use both the front and back loops of the same stitch, but in different rounds, building on what you learned in Part 8.

Why though?

Well, it allows for another dimension by allowing the layering of stitches without the bulk of front post and back post stitches.

I used this technique to create the "V" shapes in the octagon section of my Mayan pattern.

When going back to use the front loop of a stitch that has had the back loop used, poke your hook up from below – just like when you are using a front loop from a stitch that hasn't been used.

When going back to use the back loop only of a stitch that has had the front loop used, poke your hook downwards through the loop. This loop will be behind the stitches worked into the front loops.

# Why do we get stretched loops?

Look closely at the "v" of any stitch. If you pull on the front loop, the back one gets smaller and vice versa.

You are used to this happening as you work back loops only and you know that the loops settle down again once you work more stitches. The same thing happens when you work a few front loops only in a row.

The "v" on the top of a stitch is one bit of yarn but we think of the two strands of the "v" as separate parts – back and front loop. That is why you get the big loop when you work into either loop only. The act of inserting your hook into either loop and working a stitch pulls the yarn of the "v" to the back or the front, stretching it.

The difference in this example from using a back loop only is that when using only 1 stitch and coming back to it in a later round, the loop stays stretched out. The stitches either side have already been worked into, meaning the loop can't be pulled back into line. It's fine. You will not notice that long loop once your square is finished and part of a larger thing.

## Using the front loop only as a feature?

It is quite common to use the back loop only in crochet patterns as a feature. Doing so leaves a line of the unworked front loops showing, adding texture and interest as you can see in this pattern.

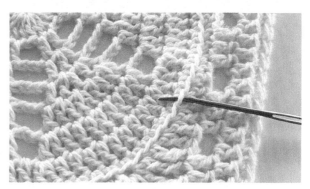

However, there is no obvious difference to the front of crochet when you use the front loop only. Sure, the loops are pulled up a little, but unlike using the back loops only, there is no discernible difference creating a feature or texture.

This photo shows 3 of the side stitches worked into the flo. You can see the 3 stitches are sitting a little taller due to the loops being pulled up, but they otherwise look very similar to the stitches worked into stitches either side.

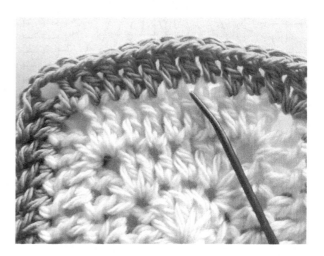

# Bob Leans On Flo

## Part Nine · UK Pattern

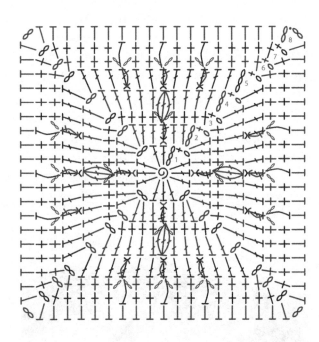

## Abbreviations

| | | |
|---|---|---|
| | cnr | corner |
| | R | Round |
| | rep | repeat |
| | sp/s | space/s |
| | st/s | stitch/es |
| | stch | starting chain |
| • | ss | slip stitch |
| ○ | ch | chain |
| + | dc | double crochet |
| T | htr | half treble crochet |
| | tr | treble crochet |
| | hdtr | half double treble crochet |
| | dtr | double treble crochet |
| | cl | cluster |
| ∩ | blo | back loop only |
| ∪ | flo | front loop only |

Begin with mc.

**R1:** ch3 (stch), 2tr, *ch2, 3tr*, rep from * to * 2x, ch1, join with dc to 3rd ch of stch.
{3 sts on each side; 4 2-ch cnr sps}

**R2:** ch3 (stch), tr over joining dc, *tr in next st, tr in blo of next st, tr in next st**, (2tr, ch2, 2tr) in 2-ch cnr sp*, rep from * to * 2x and * to ** 1x, 2tr in same sp as first sts, ch1, join with dc to 3rd ch of stch.
{7 sts on each side; 4 2-ch cnr sps}

**R3:** dc over joining dc, *dc in next 3 sts, ch2, dc in flo of R1 st below, ch2, skip 1 st, dc in next 3 sts**, (dc, ch2, dc) in 2-ch cnr sp*, rep from * to * 2x and * to ** 1x, dc in same sp as first st, ch1, join with dc to first st.
{9 sts, 2 2-ch sps on each side; 4 2ch cnr sps}

**R4:** ch3 (stch), *tr in next 4 sts, 3trcl in skipped st of R2 behind R3 sts, skip (2-ch sp, 1 st & 2-ch sp), tr in next 4 sts**, (tr, ch2, tr) in 2-ch cnr sp*, rep from * to * 2x and * to ** 1x, tr in same sp as first st, ch1, join with dc to 3rd ch of stch.
{11 sts on each side; 4 2-ch cnr sps}

**R5:** ch3 (stch), *3x [tr in next 2 sts, tr in blo of next st], tr in next 2 sts**, (tr, ch2, tr) in 2-ch cnr sp*, rep from * to * 2x and * to ** 1x, tr in same sp as first st, ch1, join with dc to 3rd ch of stch.
{13 sts on each side; 4 2-ch cnr sps}

**R6:** dc over joining dc, *dc in next 3 sts, 3x [ch2, dc in flo of R4 st below, ch2, skip 1 st, dc in next 2 sts], dc in next st**, (dc, ch2, dc) in 2-ch cnr sp*, rep from * to * 2x and * to ** 1x, dc in same sp as first st, ch1, join with dc to first st.
{15 sts, 6 2-ch sps on each side; 4 2-ch cnr sps}

**R7:** dc over joining dc, *dc in next 4 sts, 3x [htr in skipped st of R5 behind R6 sts, skip (2-ch sp, 1 st & 2-ch sp), dc in next 2 sts], dc in next 2 sts**, (dc, ch2, dc) in 2-ch cnr sp*, rep from * to * 2x and * to ** 1x, dc in same sp as first st, ch1, join with dc to first st.
{17 sts on each side; 4 2-ch cnr sps}

**R8:** ch2 (stch), *htr in next 17 sts**, (htr, ch2, htr) in 2-ch cnr sp*, rep from * to * 2x and * to ** 1x, htr in same sp as first st, ch2, join with ss to 2nd ch of stch. Fasten off.
{19 sts on each side; 4 2-ch cnr sps}

# Bob Leans On Flo

## Part Nine · US Pattern

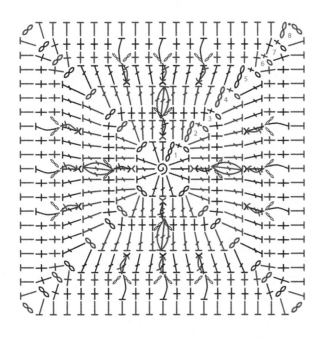

## Abbreviations

| | | |
|---|---|---|
| | cnr | corner |
| | R | Round |
| | rep | repeat |
| | sp/s | space/s |
| | st/s | stitch/es |
| | stch | starting chain |
| • | ss | slip stitch |
| ο | ch | chain |
| + | sc | single crochet |
| T | hdc | half double crochet |
| † | dc | double crochet |
| † | htr | half triple crochet |
| † | tr | triple crochet |
| ◊ | cl | cluster |
| ∩ | blo | back loop only |
| ∪ | flo | front loop only |

**Begin with mc.**

**R1:** ch3 (stch), 2dc, *ch2, 3dc*, rep from * to * 2x, ch1, join with sc to 3rd ch of stch.
{3 sts on each side; 4 2-ch cnr sps}

**R2:** ch3 (stch), dc over joining sc, *dc in next st, dc in blo of next st, dc in next st**, (2dc, ch2, 2dc) in 2-ch cnr sp*, rep from * to * 2x and * to ** 1x, 2dc in same sp as first sts, ch1, join with sc to 3rd ch of stch.
{7 sts on each side; 4 2-ch cnr sps}

**R3:** sc over joining sc, *sc in next 3 sts, ch2, sc in flo of R1 st below, ch2, skip 1 st, sc in next 3 sts**, (sc, ch2, sc) in 2-ch cnr sp*, rep from * to * 2x and * to ** 1x, sc in same sp as first st, ch1, join with sc to first st.
{9 sts, 2 2-ch sps on each side; 4 2ch cnr sps}

**R4:** ch3 (stch), *dc in next 4 sts, 3dccl in skipped st of R2 behind R3 sts, skip (2-ch sp, 1 st & 2-ch sp), dc in next 4 sts**, (dc, ch2, dc) in 2-ch cnr sp*, rep from * to * 2x and * to ** 1x, dc in same sp as first st, ch1, join with sc to 3rd ch of stch.
{11 sts on each side; 4 2-ch cnr sps}

**R5:** ch3 (stch), *3x [dc in next 2 sts, dc in blo of next st], dc in next 2 sts**, (dc, ch2, dc) in 2-ch cnr sp*, rep from * to * 2x and * to ** 1x, dc in same sp as first st, ch1, join with sc to 3rd ch of stch.
{13 sts on each side; 4 2-ch cnr sps}

**R6:** sc over joining sc, *sc in next 3 sts, 3x [ch2, sc in flo of R4 st below, ch2, skip 1 st, sc in next 2 sts], sc in next st**, (sc, ch2, sc) in 2-ch cnr sp*, rep from * to * 2x and * to ** 1x, sc in same sp as first st, ch1, join with sc to first st.
{15 sts, 6 2-ch sps on each side; 4 2-ch cnr sps}

**R7:** sc over joining sc, *sc in next 4 sts, 3x [hdc in skipped st of R5 behind R6 sts, skip (2-ch sp, 1 st & 2-ch sp), sc in next 2 sts], sc in next 2 sts**, (sc, ch2, sc) in 2-ch cnr sp*, rep from * to * 2x and * to ** 1x, sc in same sp as first st, ch1, join with sc to first st.
{17 sts on each side; 4 2-ch cnr sps}

**R8:** ch2 (stch), *hdc in next 17 sts**, (hdc, ch2, hdc) in 2-ch cnr sp*, rep from * to * 2x and * to ** 1x, hdc in same sp as first st, ch2, join with ss to 2nd ch of stch. Fasten off.
{19 sts on each side; 4 2-ch cnr sps}

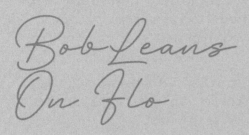

## Bob Leans On Flo

### Pattern Help

To maximize your learning, use these notes and photos to work from as you make the pattern.

If you get stuck, watch me make the pattern in the video:

 *Bob Leans On Flo video*

 *Mirrored Bob Leans On Flo video*

Prior knowledge needed from Granny Square Academy:

▷ *Back loop only*
**Part 3**

▷ *Clusters*
**Part 8**

## Round 2

In this round the middle stitch of the side is worked in the back loop only, setting us up to come back to the front loop of the same stitch in the next round.

## Round 3

After your stitches along the side and chaining 2, it's time to use the front loop left available of the Round 1 stitch.

After making the stitch in the front loop and chaining 2 again, you are instructed to skip 1 stitch. The stitch to skip is the one worked into the back loop only in Round 2, the middle stitch of the side.

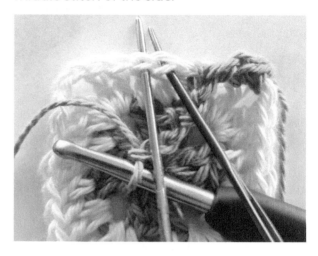

*The red needle is in the stitch to skip and the silver in the first of the last three side stitches.*

## Round 4

The fourth stitch of the side to be worked into may be a little obscured as it is the last one before you chained 2 and went down to the front loop of Round 1.

Then it is time to go back to the skipped stitch of Round 2 behind the chains and the stitch in the front loop.

After working into the Round 2 stitch, you skip the 2 chains, 1 stitch in the front loop and the second 2 chains before working a stitch into the last 4 stitches of the side.

## Round 5

Make sure you just work into the back loop only of every third stitch along the side.

## Round 6

Again you will be working into the front loops left open after the last round, just like you did in Round 3 but this time, you'll do the same thing three times along each side.

## Now...

After you've made your first square, weave in your ends, block it and then make notes in the project planner. Record:

- Yarn and hook used
- Size
- Weight

Once you've done all of that, make another one or more. If you used the video, try to make it using the chart or written pattern this time. Note down how many more you make as you go.

Well done! Time to move on to the next lesson.

R1

R2

R3

R4

R5

R6

R7

R8

# Part Ten

## Reading

## Patterns

## Spiky Sid Pattern Help

## Recap of spike stitches

Of all the patterns in the first Granny Square Academy book, Spiky Sally while being one of my favourites, caused some folks angst.

**TIP**

**Remember that pulling up a long loop when making your spike stitches means you will avoid distorting your work.**

# Spike stitches in detail

Let's play some more with spike stitches and see if I can change your mind about them if you didn't like them the first time around.

The biggest issue folks have with spike stitches is knowing where to insert your hook.

Think of the spike stitch as encasing a stitch or chain space from a previous round or rounds. It looks similar on the back and the front with two long strands of yarn encasing the stitch.

*Spiky Sally front*

*Spiky Sally back*

The pattern may vary in its instruction for spike stitches, so let's look at a few different ways you may be instructed to work a spike stitch. All these examples are UK terms.

The most common instruction will be something like this;

*"... spike dc over next st, ..."*

This means you will be working a spike stitch over the next stitch. The thing to do is look for the P of that next stitch. Look at the base of that stitch. You poke your hook in the same spot that next stitch was worked into.

The red needle is inserted in the base of the next stitch. That stitch is encased by the spike stitch, front and back.

*Spike over stitch - front*

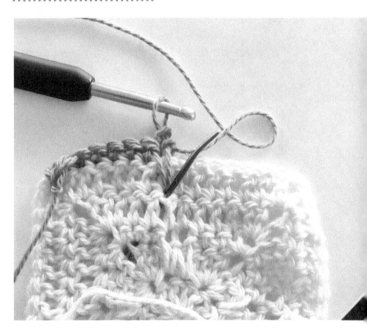

*Spike over stitch - back*

Or you may be working into stitches that were skipped in the previous round.

*"... spike dc in next 2 sts of R1 below, ..."*

You don't always encase a stitch though. You may be encasing a chain space instead of a stitch.

*"... spike dc over 1-ch sp in skipped st of R, ..."*

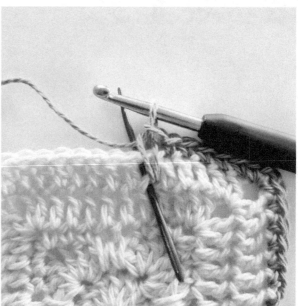

Or you may be working into a chain space instead of where a stitch was worked and be encasing more than one chain space. You could also be encasing a combination of stitches and chain spaces.

*"... spike dc in 2-ch sp of R1 below, ..."*

Another way you can work spike stitches is to make them into the space between stitches. The instruction for that may read something like this:

*"... spike dc over next st into gap between R2 sts below, ..."*

You can be instructed to work more than one spike stitch into the same stitch or space as you will see in the Spiky Sid pattern.

Spike stitches really can be used in so many ways.

# Working into spike stitches

Usually, you will be working into the top of spike stitches, under the "v" as you normally would. But there is another place you can work into.

In the pattern for this part, you will be leaving the tops of the spike stitches free and instead using the two long strands on the back to work into.

This technique creates layers in your crochet. I did this in the Spiky Sid pattern for this part.

## TIP

**When working into the long back loops of the spike stitches, make sure your hook is going through the two loops. If there are spike stitches worked consecutively, it can be harder to see the two loops you need.**

# Spiky Sid

## Part Ten · UK Pattern

## Abbreviations

| | |
|---|---|
| cnr | corner |
| R | Round |
| rep | repeat |
| sp/s | space/s |
| st/s | stitch/es |
| stch | starting chain |
| ss | slip stitch |
| ch | chain |
| dc | double crochet |
| htr | half treble crochet |
| tr | treble crochet |
| spike | spike stitch |
| | at the same time |

**Begin with mc.**

**R1:**  R1: ch3 (stch), 2tr, *ch2, 3tr*, rep from * to * 2x, ch1, join with dc to 3rd ch of stch.
{3 sts on each side; 4 2-ch cnr sps}

**R2:**  dc over joining dc, *skip 1 st, 5tr in next st, skip 1 st**, (dc, ch2, dc) in 2-ch cnr sp*, rep from * to * 2x and * to ** 1x, dc in same sp as first st, ch1, join with dc to first st.
{7 sts on each side; 4 2-ch cnr sps}

**R3:**  ch3 (stch), 2tr over joining dc, *skip 1 st, 2x [spike dc over next st, dc next st], spike dc over next st, skip 1 st**, 5tr in 2-ch cnr sp*, rep from * to * 2x and * to ** 1x, 2tr in same sp as first sts, join with ss to 3rd ch of stch.
{5 sts on each side; 4 5-st cnrs}

**R4:**  dc in same st as ss, *2x [spike dc over next st], 2x [dc in 2 loops at back of next spike st, ch1, skip 1 st], dc in 2 loops at back of next spike st, 2x [spike dc over next st]**, (dc, ch2, dc) in next st*, rep from * to * 2x and * to ** 1x, dc in same st as first st, ch1, join with dc to first st.
{9 sts, 2 1-ch sps on each side; 4 2-ch cnr sps}

**R5:**  dc over joining dc, *dc in next st, 2x [dc in 2 loops at back of next spike st], 2x [dc in next st, dc in 1-ch sp], dc in next st, 2x [dc in 2 loops at back of next spike st], dc in next st**, (dc, ch2, dc) in 2-ch cnr sp*, rep from * to * 2x and * to ** 1x, dc in same sp as first st, ch1, join with dc to first st.
{13 sts on each side; 4 2-ch cnr sps}

**R6:**  ch3 (stch), *tr in next 13 sts**, tr in 2-ch cnr sp*, rep from * to * 2x and * to ** 1x, join with ss to 3rd ch of stch.
{13 sts on each side; 4 1-st cnrs}

**R7:**  dc in same st as ss, *6x [dc in next st, spike dc over next st], dc in next st**, (dc, ch2, dc) in next st*, rep from * to * 2x and * to ** 1x, dc in same st as first st, ch1, join with dc to first st.
{15 sts on each side; 4 2-ch cnr sps}

**R8:**  ch2 (stch), *htr in next 2 sts, 6x [dc in 2 loops at back of next spike st, htr in next st], htr in next st**, (htr, ch2, htr) in 2-ch cnr sp*, rep from * to * 2x and * to ** 1x, htr in same sp as first st, ch1, join with dc to 2nd ch of stch.
{17 sts on each side; 4 2-ch cnr sps}

**R9:**  ch2 (stch), *htr in next 17 sts**, (htr, ch2, htr) in 2-ch cnr sp*, rep from * to * 2x and * to ** 1x, htr in same sp as first st, ch2, join with ss to 2nd ch of stch. Fasten off.
{19 sts on each side; 4 2-ch cnr sps}

## Spiky Sid

### Part Ten · US Pattern

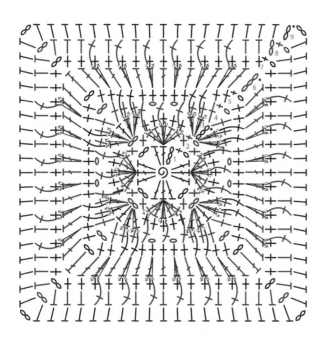

## Abbreviations

| | | |
|---|---|---|
| | cnr | corner |
| | R | Round |
| | rep | repeat |
| | sp/s | space/s |
| | st/s | stitch/es |
| | stch | starting chain |
| • | ss | slip stitch |
| ○ | ch | chain |
| + | sc | single crochet |
| T | hdc | half double crochet |
| T | dc | double crochet |
| V | spike | spike stitch |
| ⌒ | | at the same time |

Begin with mc.

**R1:** ch3 (stch), 2dc, *ch2, 3dc*, rep from * to * 2x, ch1, join with sc to 3rd ch of stch.
{3 sts on each side; 4 2-ch cnr sps}

**R2:** sc over joining sc, *skip 1 st, 5dc in next st, skip 1 st**, (sc, ch2, sc) in 2-ch cnr sp*, rep from * to * 2x and * to ** 1x, sc in same sp as first st, ch1, join with sc to first st.
{7 sts on each side; 4 2-ch cnr sps}

**R3:** ch3 (stch), 2dc over joining sc, *skip 1 st, 2x [spike sc over next st, sc next st], spike sc over next st, skip 1 st**, 5dc in 2-ch cnr sp*, rep from * to * 2x and * to ** 1x, 2dc in same sp as first sts, join with ss to 3rd ch of stch.
{5 sts on each side; 4 5-st cnrs}

**R4:** sc in same st as ss, *2x [spike sc over next st], 2x [sc in 2 loops at back of next spike st, ch1, skip 1 st], sc in 2 loops at back of next spike st, 2x [spike sc over next st]**, (sc, ch2, sc) in next st*, rep from * to * 2x and * to ** 1x, sc in same st as first st, ch1, join with sc to first st.
{9 sts, 2 1-ch sps on each side; 4 2-ch cnr sps}

**R5:** sc over joining sc, *sc in next st, 2x [sc in 2 loops at back of next spike st], 2x [sc in next st, sc in 1-ch sp], sc in next st, 2x [sc in 2 loops at back of next spike st], sc in next st**, (sc, ch2, sc) in 2-ch cnr sp*, rep from * to * 2x and * to ** 1x, sc in same sp as first st, ch1, join with sc to first st.
{13 sts on each side; 4 2-ch cnr sps}

**R6:** ch3 (stch), *dc in next 13 sts**, dc in 2-ch cnr sp*, rep from * to * 2x and * to ** 1x, join with ss to 3rd ch of stch.
{13 sts on each side; 4 1-st cnrs}

**R7:** sc in same st as ss, *6x [sc in next st, spike sc over next st], sc in next st**, (sc, ch2, sc) in next st*, rep from * to * 2x and * to ** 1x, sc in same st as first st, ch1, join with sc to first st.
{15 sts on each side; 4 2-ch cnr sps}

**R8:** ch2 (stch), *hdc in next 2 sts, 6x [sc in 2 loops at back of next spike st, hdc in next st], hdc in next st**, (hdc, ch2, hdc) in 2-ch cnr sp*, rep from * to * 2x and * to ** 1x, hdc in same sp as first st, ch1, join with sc to 2nd ch of stch.
{17 sts on each side; 4 2-ch cnr sps}

**R9:** ch2 (stch), *hdc in next 17 sts**, (hdc, ch2, hdc) in 2-ch cnr sp*, rep from * to * 2x and * to ** 1x, hdc in same sp as first st, ch2, join with ss to 2nd ch of stch. Fasten off.
{19 sts on each side; 4 2-ch cnr sps}

# Spiky Sid

## Pattern Help

To maximize your learning, use these notes and photos to work from as you make the pattern.

If you get stuck, watch me make the pattern in the video:

 *Spiky Sid video*

 *Mirrored Spiky Sid video*

Prior knowledge needed from Granny Square Academy:

▷ *Spike stitches*
   **Part 4**

## Round 2

Placing a stitch marker in your first stitch as soon as you make it will show you where to join the end of the round. And a scrap of yarn in the gap before you join will help with the start of Round 3.

## Round 3

The spike stitch fun begins! The scrap of yarn shows you where to work your 2 stitches over the joining stitch. If you left the stitch maker in the first stitch of Round 2, that is the stitch you skip.

The interesting bit is how you treat the 5 stitches in one along the side. The first, third and fifth stitches have a spike stitch worked **over** them. The second and fourth have a stitch worked **into** them. As the 5 stitches were worked into one Round 1 stitch, all of the spike stitches are worked into that same Round 1 stitch, encasing 3 of the 5 stitches.

*The silver needle is in the first stitch of the 5, This is the stitch you work your first spike stitch over, where the red needle is.*

Then, a stitch is worked into the second of the 5 before the next spike over the third stitch, in the same stitch the first spike stitch was worked.

Then there is a stitch worked in the next stitch before the third spike stitch is worked over the last of the 5 stitches, in the same stitch once more.

The corners of this round are 5 stitches in the 2-chain corner spaces.

If you find your spike legs getting twisted, at the end of the round, untwist them with your fingers.

# Round 4

It's all going on in Round 4! Just like in Round 3, some of the 5 stitches in the corners will have spike stitches worked over them. This time, the middle stitch is where the corner stitches will be worked and the 2 stitches either side have spike stitches worked over them.

After your first corner stitch, you work a spike stitch over each of the next 2 stitches, into the 2-chain space of Round 2 your Round 3 corners were worked into.

Now it's time to work on the back into the legs of the spike stitches from the last round. You will work a stitch into the back of each of the 3 spike stitches on the side and a chain between them. You will skip the stitches between the spike stitches.

Chain 1 and skip the next stitch and find the legs of the middle spike stitch on the back.

*skip this stitch*
......................

*back of next spike stitch*
......................................

And repeat that again before moving on to the spike stitches over the first 2 stitches of the 5 corner stitches.

## Round 5

Once again, you will be using the backs of the spike stitches, but this time as the spike stitches were worked next to each other, it can be harder to see the right legs of each stitch. Once you have located the first one, it's all good.

## Round 7

In this round, you will be working spike stitches as you normally would.

The first spike stitch is worked over the second stitch of the side. The red needle is pointing to the base of that stitch, where you will work your first spike stitch, and the silver needle is in the stitch you will work a stitch into. Every second stitch will be a spike stitch over the next stitch.

## Round 8

Once again, you will be using the legs on the back of the Round 7 spike stitches to work into. Every stitch between the spikes is also used.

## Now...

After you've made your first square, weave in your ends, block it and then make notes in the project planner. Record:

- Yarn and hook used
- Size
- Weight

Once you've done all of that, make another one or more. If you used the video, try to make it using the chart or written pattern this time. Note down how many more you make as you go.

Well done! Time to move on to the next lesson.

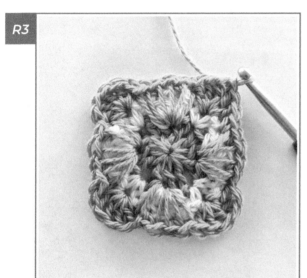

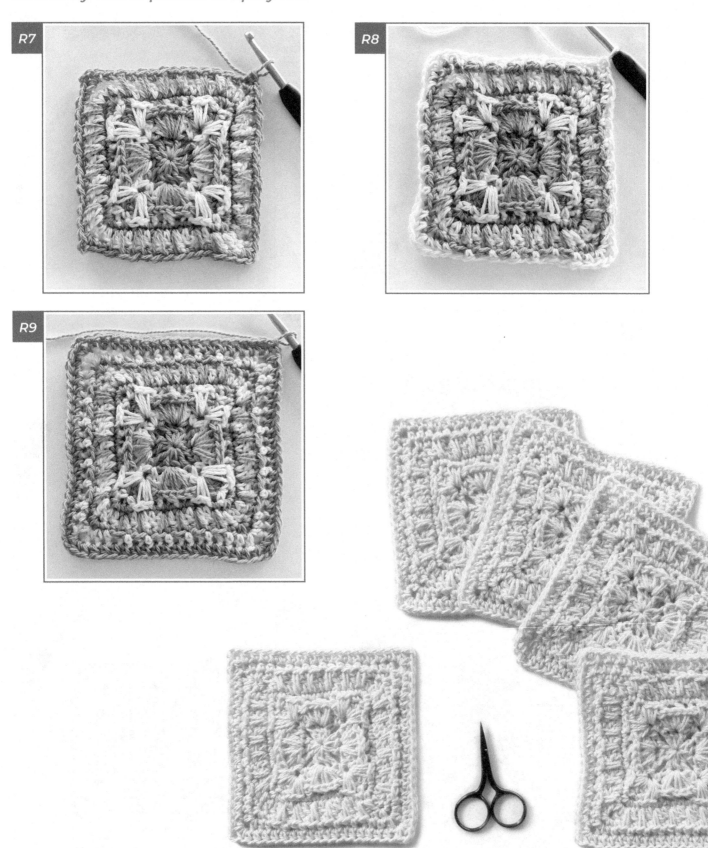

R7

R8

R9

# Part Eleven

## Reading

## Patterns

## Merge Mel Pattern Help

## Combining stitches and techniques

You have been doing this throughout both the first Granny Square Academy and this book. Now it's time to really break down what exactly you have been doing.

If you look at any of the abbreviations lists or the glossary, you will see that stitches and techniques are listed separately.

For example, if a pattern has fptr in it, the abbreviations list and/or glossary don't show fptr as an entry. Rather the stitch is listed (tr), as is the technique (fp).

| Abbreviations | |
|---|---|
| cnr | corner |
| R | Round |
| rep | repeat |
| sp/s | space/s |
| st/s | stitch/es |
| stch | starting chain |
| ss | slip stitch |
| ch | chain |
| dc | double crochet |
| htr | half treble crochet |
| tr | treble crochet |
| dtr | double treble crochet |
| fp | front post |

The first reason stitches and techniques are listed separately is that they are different things.

These are the most commonly used stitches:

| UK | US |
| --- | --- |
| chain | chain |
| double crochet | single crochet |
| half treble crochet | half double crochet |
| treble crochet | double crochet |
| double treble crochet | triple crochet |

Techniques are variations on where stitches are made and ways the stitches are made. You have learned many techniques with Granny Square Academy.

### Where to work stitches:

Back post

Front post

Back loop only

Front loop only

Loop behind V

Same stitch

Between

Skipping stitches

Turning

In front

Behind

In rounds other than the previous round

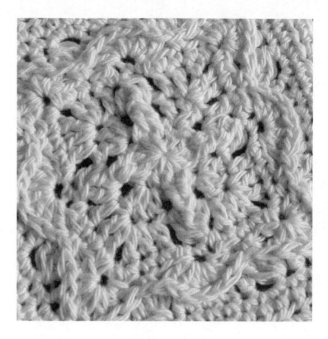

### Ways to make stitches

Clusters

Together

Spike stitches

The second reason they are listed like this is for conciseness, which at first may seem silly. Why split fptr into 2 entries? Now consider a pattern that uses fpdc, fphtr, fphdtr, fpttr as well as fptr.

In that case the list of stitches could potentially be 10 separate entries just for those stitches. One for each stitch type if it is used in the pattern as a stitch, as well as the front post version of the same stitches, in addition to all the other stitch and technique combinations used in the pattern.

Listing the stitches and techniques separately means the list is shorter.

# How to work out what to do

Brevity is important in crochet instructions. The more words there are, the harder they are to follow. That is why the instruction for a front post treble is written as fptr.

fptr is a simple example and it's easy to work out what to do.

If you're confronted with a longer stitch and technique combination, you apply the same method: break each part of the instruction down.

Let's look at a few examples from some of my more advanced patterns.

### "... tr in blo of R24 st behind R25 sts, ..."

This one instruction uses one stitch and three techniques.

The stitch is **tr**, treble crochet.

The first technique is the treble crochet is worked into the **blo**, back loop only.

The second technique is that the blo is from a stitch of **R24** 2 rounds previous to the current round.

And the last technique is that the treble crochet is worked **behind** R25 sts, the previous round's stitches.

### "... fptr3tog over next 5 sts skipping 2nd and 4th sts, ..."

This instruction uses one stitch and three techniques.

The stitch used is a **tr**, treble crochet.

The first technique is the tr is a **fp**, front post.

It's not a simple treble though, it is **3tog**, 3 trebles worked together.

And the three legs of the front post treble 3 **together** are worked over the next 5 stitches, but the second and fourth of those 5 stitches are skipped.

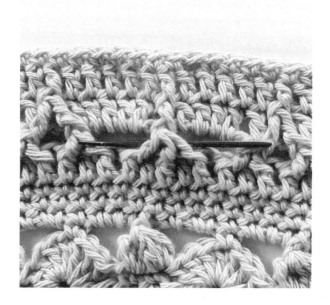

*"... **fpdtr3tog** over next 3 R4 sts, ..."*

This one instruction also uses one stitch type and three techniques.

In this case, the stitch is a **dtr** = double treble crochet.

The first technique is **fp**, so the stitch you work is a front post version of the stitch.

But it is not a single dtr. It is 3 stitches worked **together** as a together cluster.

And this 3-stitch front post double treble cluster is worked over 3 stitches of an earlier round, **Round 4**.

TIP

**When confronted with a long complex stitch and technique combination, break it down and write it out if you need to. EG: fptr3tog = front post treble crochet 3 together**

# Merge Mel

## Part Eleven · UK Pattern

## Abbreviations

| | | |
|---|---|---|
| | cnr | corner |
| | R | Round |
| | rep | repeat |
| | sp/s | space/s |
| | st/s | stitch/es |
| | stch | starting chain |
| · | ss | slip stitch |
| o | ch | chain |
| + | dc | double crochet |
| T | htr | half treble crochet |
| T | tr | treble crochet |
| A | tog | together |
| ∨ | lbv | loop behind v |
| | hdtr | half double treble crochet |
| | dtr | double treble crochet |
| **[RS]** | RS | right side |
| **[WS]** | WS | wrong side |
| ↄ | fp | front post |

Begin with mc.

**R1:** ch3 (stch), 11tr, join with ss to 3rd ch of stch.
{12 sts}

**R2:** ch3 (stch), tr in same st as ss, *ch1, fptr2tog over next 2 sts, ch1**, 3tr in next st*, rep from * to * 2x and * to ** 1x, tr in same st as first sts, join with ss to 3rd ch of stch.
{1 st, 2 1-ch sps on each side; 4 3-st cnrs}

**R3:** ch3 (stch), tr in same st as ss, *tr in next st, ch1, tr3tog with middle st as fp over (1-ch sp, next st & 1-ch sp), ch1, tr in next st**, (2tr, ch2, 2tr) in next st*, rep from * to * 2x and * to ** 1x, 2tr in same st as first sts, ch1, join with dc to 3rd ch of stch.
{7 sts, 2 1-ch sps on each side; 4 2-ch cnr sps}

**R4:** dc over joining dc, *dc in next 3 sts, dc in 1-ch sp, dc in next st, dc in 1-ch sp, dc in next 3 sts**, (dc, ch2, dc) in 2-ch cnr sp*, rep from * to * 2x and * to ** 1x, dc in same sp as first st, ch1, join with dc to first st.
{11 sts on each side; 4 2-ch cnr sps}

**R5:** ch3 (stch), 3tr over joining dc, *skip 2 sts, dc in next st, skip 2 sts, 7tr in next st, skip 2 sts, dc in next st, skip 2 sts**, 7tr in 2-ch cnr sp*, rep from * to * 2x and * to ** 1x, 3tr in same sp as first sts, join with ss to 3rd ch of stch.
{9 sts on each side; 4 7-st cnrs}

**R6:** dc in same st as ss, *dc in lbv of next st, htr in lbv of next st, tr3tog in lbv of next 3 sts, htr in lbv of next st, dc in lbv of next 3 sts, htr in lbv of next st, tr3tog in lbv of next 3 sts, htr in lbv of next st, dc in lbv of next st**, (dc, ch2, dc) in next st*, rep from * to * 2x and * to ** 1x, dc in same st as first st, ch1, join with dc to first st.
{13 sts on each side; 4 2-ch cnr sps}

**R7:** dc over joining dc, *dc in next 3 sts, 2dc in next st, dc in next 5 sts, 2dc in next st, dc in next 3 sts**, (dc, ch2, dc) in 2-ch cnr sp*, rep from * to * 2x and * to ** 1x, dc in same sp as first st, ch1, join with dc to first st.
{17 sts on each side; 4 2-ch cnr sps}

**R8:** [WS] turn, ch2 (stch), *htr in next 17 sts**, (htr, ch2, htr) in 2-ch cnr sp*, rep from * to * 2x and * to ** 1x, htr in same sp as first st, ch1, join with dc to 2nd ch of stch.
{19 sts on each side; 4 2-ch cnr sps}

**R9:** [RS] turn, dc over 1-ch, *dc in next 19 sts**, (dc, ch2, dc) in 2-ch cnr sp*, rep from * to * 2x and * to ** 1x, dc in same sp as first st, ch2, join with ss to first st. Fasten off.
{21 sts on each side; 4 2-ch cnr sps}

# Merge Mel

## Part Eleven · US Pattern

## Abbreviations

| | | |
|---|---|---|
| | cnr | corner |
| | R | Round |
| | rep | repeat |
| | sp/s | space/s |
| | st/s | stitch/es |
| | stch | starting chain |
| • | ss | slip stitch |
| o | ch | chain |
| + | sc | single crochet |
| T | hdc | half double crochet |
| T | dc | double crochet |
| A | tog | together |
| v | lbv | loop behind v |
| T | htr | half triple crochet |
| T | tr | triple crochet |
| [RS] | RS | right side |
| [WS] | WS | wrong side |
| ↄ | fp | front post |

**Begin with mc.**

**R1:** ch3 (stch), 11dc, join with ss to 3rd ch of stch.
{12 sts}

**R2:** ch3 (stch), dc in same st as ss, *ch1, fpdc2tog over next 2 sts, ch1**, 3dc in next st*, rep from * to * 2x and * to ** 1x, dc in same st as first sts, join with ss to 3rd ch of stch.
{1 st, 2 1-ch sps on each side; 4 3-st cnrs}

**R3:** ch3 (stch), dc in same st as ss, *dc in next st, ch1, dc3tog with middle st as fp over (1-ch sp, next st & 1-ch sp), ch1, dc in next st**, (2dc, ch2, 2dc) in next st*, rep from * to * 2x and * to ** 1x, 2dc in same st as first sts, ch1, join with sc to 3rd ch of stch.
{7 sts, 2 1-ch sps on each side; 4 2-ch cnr sps}

**R4:** sc over joining sc, *sc in next 3 sts, sc in 1-ch sp, sc in next st, sc in 1-ch sp, sc in next 3 sts**, (sc, ch2, sc) in 2-ch cnr sp*, rep from * to * 2x and * to ** 1x, sc in same sp as first st, ch1, join with sc to first st.
{11 sts on each side; 4 2-ch cnr sps}

**R5:** ch3 (stch), 3dc over joining sc, *skip 2 sts, sc in next st, skip 2 sts, 7dc in next st, skip 2 sts, sc in next st, skip 2 sts**, 7dc in 2-ch cnr sp*, rep from * to * 2x and * to ** 1x, 3dc in same sp as first sts, join with ss to 3rd ch of stch.
{9 sts on each side; 4 7-st cnrs}

**R6:** sc in same st as ss, *sc in lbv of next st, hdc in lbv of next st, dc3tog in lbv of next 3 sts, hdc in lbv of next st, sc in lbv of next 3 sts, hdc in lbv of next st, dc3tog in lbv of next 3 sts, hdc in lbv of next st, sc in lbv of next st**, (sc, ch2, sc) in next st*, rep from * to * 2x and * to ** 1x, sc in same st as first st, ch1, join with sc to first st.
{13 sts on each side; 4 2-ch cnr sps}

**R7:** sc over joining sc, *sc in next 3 sts, 2sc in next st, sc in next 5 sts, 2sc in next st, sc in next 3 sts**, (sc, ch2, sc) in 2-ch cnr sp*, rep from * to * 2x and * to ** 1x, sc in same sp as first st, ch1, join with sc to first st.
{17 sts on each side; 4 2-ch cnr sps}

**R8:** **[WS]** turn, ch2 (stch), *hdc in next 17 sts**, (hdc, ch2, hdc) in 2-ch cnr sp*, rep from * to * 2x and * to ** 1x, hdc in same sp as first st, ch1, join with sc to 2nd ch of stch.
{19 sts on each side; 4 2-ch cnr sps}

**R9:** **[RS]** turn, sc over 1-ch, *sc in next 19 sts**, (sc, ch2, sc) in 2-ch cnr sp*, rep from * to * 2x and * to ** 1x, sc in same sp as first st, ch2, join with ss to first st. Fasten off.
{21 sts on each side; 4 2-ch cnr sps}

# Merge Mel

## Pattern Help

To maximize your learning, use these notes and photos to work from as you make the pattern.

If you get stuck, watch me make the pattern in the video:

 *Merge Mel video*

 *Mirrored Merge Mel video*

Prior knowledge needed from Granny Square Academy:

▷ *Front posts*
  **Part 6**

▷ *Clusters*
  **Part 8**

▷ *Together stitches*
  **Part 9**

Prior knowledge needed from Granny Square Academy 2:

▷ *lbv*
  **Part 1**

▷ *Turning*
  **Part 5**

## Round 2

This round has your first combined stitch and technique instruction. The middle 2 stitches of the side are worked together into 1 stitch as front posts.

That means each leg of the 2together is worked as a front post.

You begin your 2together here:

And complete the stitch with another leg around the front post of the next stitch:

## Round 3

Now this is where things get interesting! Along the side, you will be making a 3-together stitch, but where you work each leg of the stitch is different.

The first leg in in the 1-chain space, the second leg is a front post around the together cluster of Round 2 and the last leg is in the 1-chain space on the other side of the cluster. The silver needles show the 1-chain spaces and the red needle where to work the front post leg.

## Round 5

Round 5 is made up of sets of 7 stitches with a small stitch in between the sets of 7. 2 stitches are skipped between the small stitches and sets of 7.

Your set of 7 stitches along the side should fall in the stitch that is in the 3-together stitch of Round 3.

Even the corners are sets of 7 stitches, worked into the 2-chain corner spaces.

## Round 6

This is the last round that you will combine stitches and techniques. All stitches along the sides in this round are worked into the loop behind v. The interesting bit is where you work a 3-together stitch in the lbv of 3 stitches.

The middle leg of the 3-together stitch should fall in the lbv of the small stitch between the sets of 7 stitches. The red needle is indicating that lbv.

## Round 7

The only thing a little different about this round is that the 3-together stitches of Round 6 have 2 small stitches worked into them.

## Now...

After you've made your first square, weave in your ends, block it and then make notes in the project planner. Record:

- Yarn and hook used
- Size
- Weight

Once you've done all of that, make another one or more. If you used the video, try to make it using the chart or written pattern this time. Note down how many more you make as you go.

Well done! Time to move on to the next lesson.

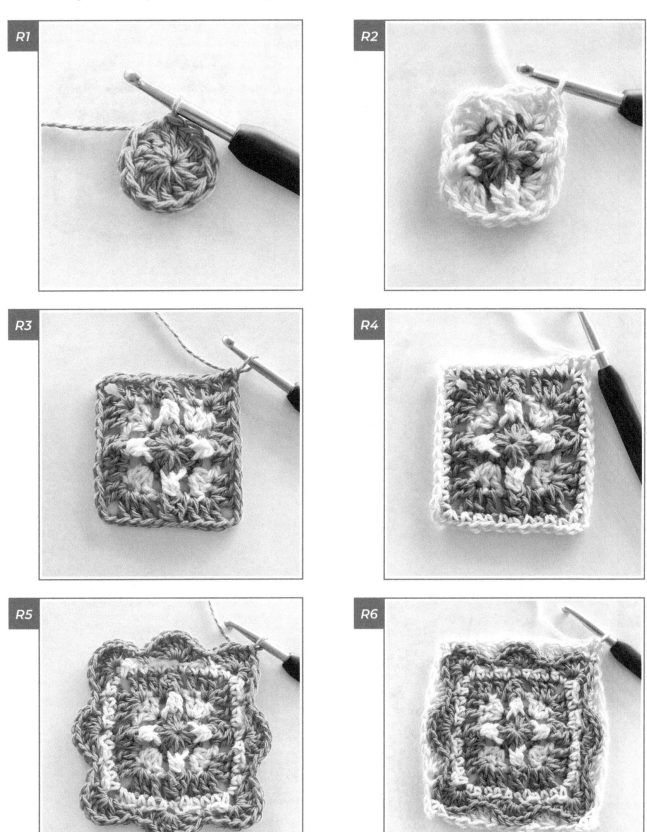

R7

R8

[RS]

R8

[WS]

R9

# Part Twelve

## Reading

## Patterns

## Coalesce Chris Pattern Help

And so we come to the last part of this instalment of Granny Square Academy.

## *That big hole problem*

There are times when making a larger stitch or large stitch cluster that the circle part of the P of the stitch or cluster can seem too big compared to other large stitches. It usually happens after making some chain and/or skipping some stitches.

A lot of the time, like in the Coalesce Chris pattern, that larger hole won't show up once the square is completed due to what happens in later rounds.

> **TIP**
>
> **Don't judge your stitches in isolation. Look at them at the end of the round or after the subsequent round as any issues you see may be resolved.**

But sometimes, it may stand out like a sore thumb to you. So how can you avoid it? It's tricky. The only way I have found is to hold very firmly to all wraps on your hook – the ones you make at the start of the stitch before you insert your hook anywhere – as you make the stitch.

The larger than usual hole forms due to your yarn overs slipping as you work the stitch. It's not usually an issue when making stitches next to each other, as the yarn is anchored firmly in the previous stitch. When you have chains or are moving across a lot of stitches before making a large stitch or large stitch cluster, there is a lot more movement in the yarn overs.

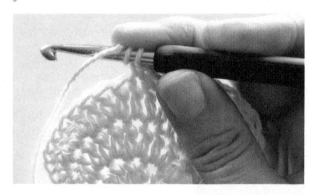

How awkward it is to hold those initial yarn overs will depend on how you hold your hook. You may need to change your hold to make it possible to firmly hold the yarn overs.

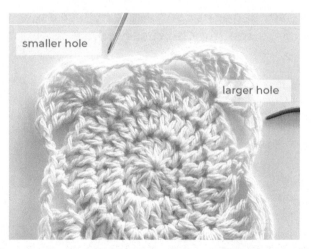

smaller hole

larger hole

# Planning a project

You can use granny squares to make lots of things. Blankets are the obvious choice, but you can also make cushion covers, scarves, cowls, garments – whatever you like.

A bit of planning will help you make your project a pleasure to make. If you want to make the sampler blanket I made, you will find the details on page 194.

## Step 1

Choose what you will make and the approximate size you want it to be.

### Example

I want to make a lap blanket, a bit over a metre across (40 inches). I want to use a mix of granny squares that are around 15 centimetres (6 inches) across. I will use one colour.

I like a slightly rectangular shape, so a grid of 7 x 8 squares will give me a blanket about 106 x 121 centimetres (42 x 48 inches).

## Step 2

Choose the patterns to use. Different granny square patterns can use significantly different amounts of yarn. Note how much yarn each one uses and how many of each to make.

If using more than one colour, working out the total yarn needed for each pattern gives you a starting point to calculate individual colour needs.

To be really precise, you can make each pattern once in your planned colours and keep track of how much of each colour you use by weighing your ball of yarn before and after using each colour.

*Example*

I will use 5 patterns and I need 56 squares.

| Pattern | Yarn | Number to make | Total yarn needed |
|---|---|---|---|
| 1 | 10 grams | 10 | 100 grams |
| 2 | 18 grams | 12 | 216 grams |
| 3 | 15 grams | 12 | 180 grams |
| 4 | 12 grams | 10 | 120 grams |
| 5 | 15 grams | 12 | 180 grams |
| | Total | 56 | 796 grams |
| Add 20% for joining and border | | | 955 grams |

Add extra to allow for joining and the border I like to add between 10 and 20 percent. The larger your project, the more you should allow. In this case, approximately 960 grams of yarn will be needed.

## Step 3

Choose your layout. You can do this before you start or once your squares are made.

There is no right or wrong here. If you like to see patterns and order, choose a layout that pleases you, making patterns with the different granny squares or colours used.

Or go completely random with your placement.

Once you are happy with your layout, take a photo and refer to it often as you join. It is very easy to flip a row and alter your planned layout drastically.

**TIP**

**If you have a mix of solid and lacy patterns, place the lacy ones away from the edges.**

## Step 4

Choose your joining method and border to finish it off.

There are many joining methods around and a few are covered next.

When it comes to adding a border, you can choose a simple frame of a few rounds of the most common stitches or get fancy with complex stitches and techniques. I like to keep things simple, so the granny square patterns are the hero.

There are entire books devoted to borders.

I have included a simple border pattern for you on page 192.

**NOTE**

**If substituting yarn from what a pattern states, matching yardage is the best way. Compare the metres/yards per gram/ounce. A close match will ensure you need a similar amount and get a close result in size.**

# Joining methods

All of the following joining methods will work to join squares with different stitch counts.

As long as the squares are the same physical size, the stitch count can vary substantially, and the squares can still be joined.

Take this extreme example. These two patterns are 12 inch squares. The stitch count for one is 34 and the other 51. And yet that stitch count difference of 17 stitches was easily accommodated by the joining. It is flat and even.

### TIP

**Refer to the table on page 191 when joining to quickly see the stitch counts of the patterns in this book.**

## Dc/sc on back join

I like to double/single crochet (UK/US) my squares together with the right sides held together through both loops of the stitches of each square.

# Dc/sc on front join

This is done the same way as the dc/sc on back join, but the squares are held with wrong sides together. Joining this way leaves a ridge on the front.

If joining this way, be mindful of joining squares so the ridge leans the same way on all joins.

Instead of joining the squares into strips then joining the strips, join the squares all the way across your project. When you pick up each new set of two squares, be mindful of keeping your tension tight between the sets of squares.

Then join the opposite way across whole rows.

## Slip stitch blo on back join

Hold the squares right sides together and slip stitch them together using the outer loops of the stitches on both squares.

Joining in this way leaves a neat line on the edge of each square, just like using blo in a pattern leaves a line.

How you treat the corner spaces is up to you. You can place a stitch in the corner stitch like the dc/sc join or you can use the back strand of the chain. I used the corner space in this example.

## Zipper join

This join is a bit more fiddly to do, but also has a great look on the front. You get a row of "v" shapes between the squares. It is done essentially the same as the Slip stitch blo on back join, but is done with the squares laying face up side by side.

Join your squares all the way across your project instead of into strips to be joined, being mindful to start your next row in the same direction.

I used the back strand of the chains in the corners in this example.

If you find your nice flat squares become buckled and wobbly after joining, try the join again using a larger hook. Slip stitch joins in particular can be very tight, causing the pulling you see here.

*too tight slip stitch join*

*flat join*

There are many ways to join granny squares and I have touched on just a few here. Spend some time on the internet searching, and you will find many more.

## Putting it all together

The pattern for this part is all about you applying knowledge learned. I encourage you to try the pattern using just the written pattern and chart before looking at the help section or the video. I know you can do it. Break it down, take it step by step.

Try out some of the options you have read about like using a false stitch as part of a cluster as well as instead of the chain 3 starting chain.

*Coalesce Chris*

## Part Twelve · UK Pattern

### Abbreviations

| | | |
|---|---|---|
| | cnr | corner |
| | R | Round |
| | rep | repeat |
| | sp/s | space/s |
| | st/s | stitch/es |
| | stch | starting chain |
| • | ss | slip stitch |
| ○ | ch | chain |
| + | dc | double crochet |
| T | htr | half treble crochet |
| T | tr | treble crochet |
| T | dtr | double treble crochet |
| S | stdg | standing |
| ↄ | bp | back post |
| ↄ | fp | front post |
| | cl | cluster |

Begin with mc with a long tail.

**R1:** ch3 (stch), 23tr, join with ss to 3rd ch of stch. Fasten off.
{24 sts}

**R2:** Don't work a false st. Attach with fpss around any st, ch3 (stch), fptr around next 23 sts, join with inv join to first true st.
{24 sts}

**R3:** Attach with stdg tr into any R1 st behind R2 sts, *2tr in next R1 st**, tr in next R1 st*, rep from * to * 10x and * to ** 1x, join with ss to first st.
{36 sts}

**R4:** dc in same st as ss, ch2, dc in next R2 st below in front of R3 sts, *ch2, skip 2 sts**, dc in next st, ch2, skip 1 st of R2, dc in next R2 st*, rep from * to * 10x and * to ** 1x, join with ss to first st.
{24 sts, 24 2-ch sps}

**R5:** ch1, bpdc around same st as ss, *2tr in next R3 st behind R4 sts, tr in next R3 st behind R4 sts, skip (2-ch sp, 1 st, 2-ch sp)**, bpdc around next st*, rep from * to * 10x and * to ** 1x, join with ss to first st.
{48 sts}

**R6:** dc in same st as ss, dc in next 47 sts, join with ss to first st.
{48 sts}

**R7:** ch4 (stch), 2dtrcl in same st as ss, *ch2, 3dtrcl in next st, skip 2 sts, dc in next 5 sts, skip 2 sts, 3dtrcl in next st, ch2**, 3dtrcl in next st*, rep from * to * 2x and * to ** 1x, join with ss to top of 2dtrcl.
{7 sts, 2 2-ch sps on each side; 4 1-st cnrs}

**R8:** 2dc in same st as ss, *2dc in 2-ch sp, 2dc in next st, dc in next 5 sts, 2dc in next st, 2dc in 2-ch sp**, (2dc, ch2, 2dc) in next st*, rep from * to * 2x and * to ** 1x, 2dc in same st as first sts, ch1, join with dc to first st.
{17 sts on each side; 4 2-ch cnr sps}

**R9:** ch2 (stch), *htr in next 17 sts**, (htr, ch2, htr) in 2-ch cnr sp*, rep from * to * 2x and * to ** 1x, htr in same sp as first st, ch2, join with ss to 2nd ch of stch. Fasten off.
{19 sts on each side; 4 2-ch cnr sps}

# Coalesce Chris

## Part Twelve · US Pattern

## Abbreviations

| | | |
|---|---|---|
| | cnr | corner |
| | R | Round |
| | rep | repeat |
| | sp/s | space/s |
| | st/s | stitch/es |
| | stch | starting chain |
| • | ss | slip stitch |
| ○ | ch | chain |
| + | sc | single crochet |
| T | hdc | half double crochet |
| ϯ | dc | double crochet |
| ϯ | tr | triple crochet |
| s | stdg | standing |
| ᴗ | bp | back post |
| ᴗ | fp | front post |
| ⬥ | cl | cluster |

Begin with mc with a long tail.

**R1:** ch3 (stch), 23dc, join with ss to 3rd ch of stch. Fasten off.
{24 sts}

**R2:** Don't work a false st. Attach with fpss around any st, ch3 (stch), fpdc around next 23 sts, join with inv join to first true st.
{24 sts}

**R3:** Attach with stdg dc into any R1 st behind R2 sts, *2dc in next R1 st**, dc in next R1 st*, rep from * to * 10x and * to ** 1x, join with ss to first st.
{36 sts}

**R4:** sc in same st as ss, ch2, sc in next R2 st below in front of R3 sts, *ch2, skip 2 sts**, sc in next st, ch2, skip 1 st of R2, sc in next R2 st*, rep from * to * 10x and * to ** 1x, join with ss to first st.
{24 sts, 24 2-ch sps}

**R5:** ch1, bpsc around same st as ss, *2dc in next R3 st behind R4 sts, dc in next R3 st behind R4 sts, skip (2-ch sp, 1 st, 2-ch sp)**, bpsc around next st*, rep from * to * 10x and * to ** 1x, join with ss to first st.
{48 sts}

**R6:** sc in same st as ss, sc in next 47 sts, join with ss to first st.
{48 sts}

**R7:** ch4 (stch), 2trcl in same st as ss, *ch2, 3trcl in next st, skip 2 sts, sc in next 5 sts, skip 2 sts, 3trcl in next st, ch2**, 3trcl in next st*, rep from * to * 2x and * to ** 1x, join with ss to top of 2trcl.
{7 sts, 2 2-ch sps on each side; 4 1-st cnrs}

**R8:** 2sc in same st as ss, *2sc in 2-ch sp, 2sc in next st, sc in next 5 sts, 2sc in next st, 2sc in 2-ch sp**, (2sc, ch2, 2sc) in next st*, rep from * to * 2x and * to ** 1x, 2sc in same st as first sts, ch1, join with sc to first st.
{17 sts on each side; 4 2-ch cnr sps}

**R9:** ch2 (stch), *hdc in next 17 sts**, (hdc, ch2, hdc) in 2-ch cnr sp*, rep from * to * 2x and * to ** 1x, hdc in same sp as first st, ch2, join with ss to 2nd ch of stch. Fasten off.
{19 sts on each side; 4 2-ch cnr sps}

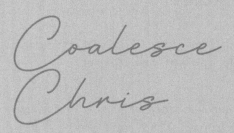

Pattern Help

To maximize your learning, use these notes and photos to work from as you make the pattern.

If you get stuck, watch me make the pattern in the video:

 *Coalesce Chris video*

*Mirrored Coalesce Chris video*

Prior knowledge needed from Granny Square Academy:

▷ *All parts of GSA and this book*

A note about this pattern. The centre is essentially the same as the Sol pattern from Granny Square Flair, but it is constructed differently and the squaring off is different.

*Sol*
· · · ·

*Coalesce*
*Chris*
· · · · · · · · · · ·

# Round 1

The pattern begins with the instruction to make a magic circle with a long tail. The reason being, there are 24 stitches in the first round. If you don't leave a long enough tail, you won't leave yourself enough to weave in properly.

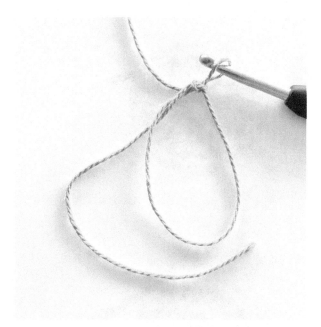

When it is time to pull the magic circle closed, you will find the next rounds easier if you leave a hole in the centre as I did in the one colour version. If you don't like the hole, you can pull it tighter once you've finished.

## Round 2

Once you get your yarn re-attached, this is an easy round. As the round ends with an invisible join, you will need to start by attaching your yarn to the front post of any stitch with a slip stitch, then chaining 3.

## Round 3

No stitches of Round 2 are used at all. All stitches are worked into the Round 1 stitches behind Round 2. Fold the Round 2 stitches forward to expose the Round 1 stitches.

## Round 4

Now we make the sun points! This is done by working alternatively between Rounds 2 and 3. You will skip 1 stitch between the Round 2 stitches and skip 2 stitches between the Round 3 stitches.

The first stitch into Round 2 is worked into the stitch slightly to the left of the Round 3 stitch you begin in (slightly right for left-handers).

Then you chain 2 and skip 2 stitches of Round 3 to work a stitch here:

After chaining 2 again, skip 1 stitch of Round 2 to work your next stitch:

## Round 5

At the start of Round 5, you are instructed to chain 1. Note it does not say (stch) after that chain 1. That means the chain 1 is not counted as a stitch. Instead, it is an aid to help you make your first back post stitch around the same stitch as your slip stitch was worked into at the end of Round 4.

Then you will be working into the Round 3 stitches between the Round 4 stitches.

## Round 7

The start of Round 7 says to chain 4 as the starting chain, then to make a 2-large stitch cluster. All the other corners are a 3-large stitch cluster. Try beginning with most steps of a false stitch to make a real 3-stitch cluster from the start.

Begin your false stitch by pulling up a longer loop and wrapping that loop twice around your hook, then yarn over and pull under the loop, yarn over and pull through the next 2 loops. Stop when you still have 2 loops on your hook, then complete the cluster as normal.

> **NOTE**
>
> **If you do make the starting chain at the start, join to the top of the 2-stitch cluster instead of the 4th chain of the starting chain, as that will help hide the starting chain.**

## Now...

After you've made your first square, weave in your ends, block it and then make notes in the project planner. Record:

- Yarn and hook used
- Size
- Weight

Once you've done all of that, make another one or more. If you used the video, try to make it using the chart or written pattern this time. Note down how many more you make as you go.

Well done! You have completed all lessons!

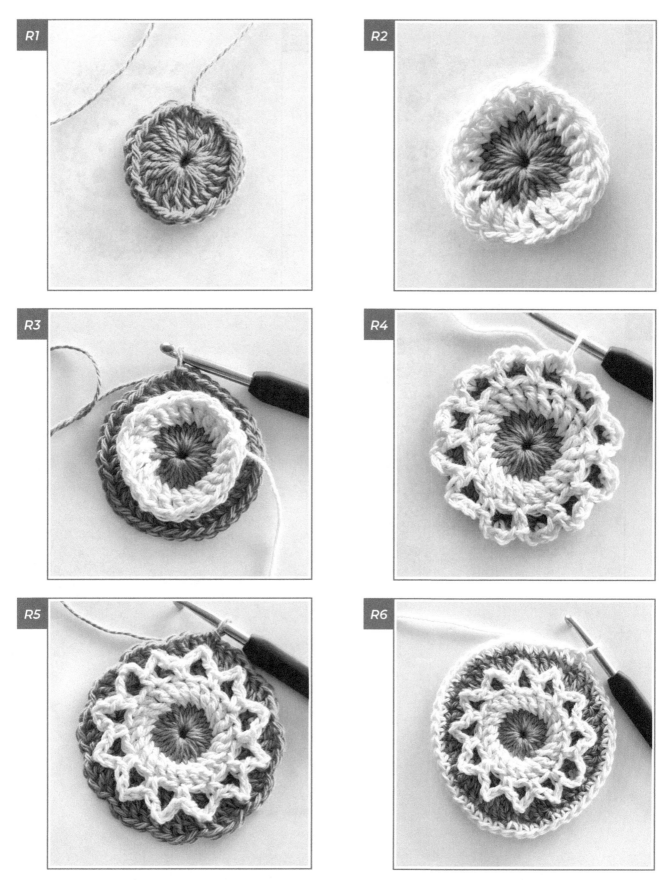

R7

R8

R9

# What's Next?

Having worked through both Granny Square Academy and Granny Square Academy 2, the crochet world is your oyster.

You now have the skills to try any pattern and succeed.

Here are some ideas of what you could do:

- Make a few squares and test the different joining methods in this book to see which you like as well as researching and trying other ways.
- Try planning your own project of Granny Square Academy patterns using the Project Planner on page 190 and the tips in Part 12.
- Join your sample squares into an item – a scarf, a cowl, a cushion cover, or a blanket and add the border on page 192.
- Make a sampler blanket like I did, but make it your own by changing the patterns to the ones you like.
- Plan a project using squares from other sources using the skills you now have.

I wish you luck for your crochet adventures. You will make amazing things, I know it.

xx *Shelley*

# Project Planner

START DATE _____

HOOK SIZE _____

UK OR US TERMS _____

NOTES _____

_____

_____

_____

YARN SOURCE _____

YARN NAME _____

YARN BRAND _____

YARN COLOUR _____

NO. BALLS PURCHASED _____

METRES/YARDS PER BALL (A) _____

GRAMS/OUNCES PER BALL (B) _____

YARDAGE* (A÷B=C) _____

*Needed if substituting yarn

| | Square size unblocked/blocked | Square weight (D) | No. to make (E) | Total Weight for Project (DxE=F) |
|---|---|---|---|---|
| Look Behind Vivien | / | | | |
| Tall Taylor | / | | | |
| Billie Between | / | | | |
| Invisible Jesse | / | | | |
| Turning Terry | / | | | |
| Same Same Sam | / | | | |
| Popcorn Perry | / | | | |
| Other Round Ricky | / | | | |
| Bob Leans On Flo | / | | | |
| Spiky Sid | / | | | |
| Merge Mel | / | | | |
| Coalesce Chris | / | | | |
| | | | Subtotal | |
| | | Add 10 to 20% for joining and border | | |
| | | | Total | |

# Pattern List

Use this list of the twelve patterns to work out your yarn needs for your own projects. When you come to join your granny squares, refer to the stitch counts.

Bendigo Woollen Mills 8 ply cotton was used to make the samples using a 4.5 mm hook. The yardage for this yarn is 485 metres per 200 gram ball, (2.425 metres per gram).

| Pattern | Grams 8 ply cotton | Stitch count |
|---|---|---|
| Look Behind Vivien | 12 | 19 |
| Tall Taylor | 13 | 21 |
| Billie Between | 14 | 19 |
| Invisible Jesse | 15 | 20 |
| Turning Terry | 12 | 20 |
| Same Same Sam | 13 | 20 |
| Popcorn Perry | 17 | 19 |
| Other Round Ricky | 14 | 21 |
| Bob Leans On Flo | 12 | 19 |
| Spiky Sid | 16 | 19 |
| Merge Mel | 14 | 21 |
| Coalesce Chris | 15 | 19 |

*Look Behind Vivien*  *Tall Taylor*  *Billie Between*  *Invisible Jesse*  *Turning Terry*  *Same Same Sam*

*Popcorn Perry*  *Other Round Ricky*  *Bob Leans On Flo*  *Spiky Sid*  *Merge Mel*  *Coalesce Chris*

# Border

A simple, framing border pattern. If you are making a sampler blanket of many different squares, your stitch counts could be different for every side.

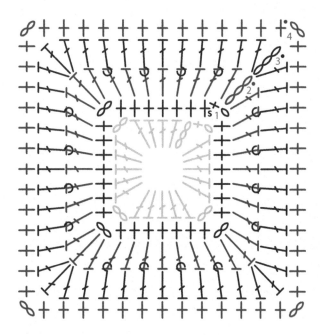

R1: Attach yarn with a stdg dc to any 2-ch cnr sp, *dc in each st on side, working a dc in each 2-ch sp and join**, (dc, ch2, dc) in 2-ch cnr sp*, rep from * to * 2x and * to ** 1x, dc in same sp as first st, ch1, join with dc to first st.

Odd number of stitches needed for this round. If you have an even number, skip the first stitch of the side.

R2: ch3 (stch), tr over joining dc, * tr in each st on side**, 3tr in 2-ch cnr sp*, rep from * to * 2x & * to ** 1x, tr in same sp as first sts, join with ss to 3rd ch of stch.

R3: ch3 (stch), tr in same st as ss, *as many times as needed along side [tr in next st, fptr around next st], tr in last st**, 3tr in next st*, rep from * to * 2x & * to ** 1x, tr in same st as first sts, join with ss to 3rd ch of stch.

R4: dc in same st as ss, *dc in each st along side**, (dc, ch2, dc) in next st*, rep from * to * 2x & * to ** 1x, dc in same st as first st, ch2, join with ss to first st. Fasten off.

## US terms

**R1:** Attach yarn with a stdg sc to any 2-ch cnr sp, *sc in each st on side, working a sc in each 2-ch sp and join**, (sc, ch2, sc) in 2-ch cnr sp*, rep from * to * 2x and * to ** 1x, sc in same sp as first st, ch1, join with sc to first st.

Odd number of stitches needed from here. If you have an even number, skip the first stitch of the side.

**R2:** ch3 (stch), dc over joining sc, * dc in each st on side**, 3dc in 2-ch cnr sp*, rep from * to * 2x & * to ** 1x, dc in same sp as first sts, join with ss to 3rd ch of stch.

**R3:** ch3 (stch), dc in same st as ss, *as many times as needed along side [dc in next st, fpdc around next st], dc in last st**, 3dc in next st*, rep from * to * 2x & * to ** 1x, dc in same st as first sts, join with ss to 3rd ch of stch.

**R4:** sc in same st as ss, *sc in each st along side**, (sc, ch2, sc) in next st*, rep from * to * 2x & * to ** 1x, sc in same st as first st, ch2, join with ss to first st. Fasten off.

# Sampler Blanket Project

Here are all the details of the sampler blanket I made using all twelve patterns. If you use different patterns, your yarn needs will also change. Refer to the Pattern List on page 191 for the yarn needed for each square.

▷ *Bendigo Woollen Mills Cotton*

**Fibre:**
100% cotton

**Weight:**
8 ply/DK/light worsted

**Yardage:**
485 metres/530 yards per 200 grams

**Colour:**
Parchment

**Number of balls:**
4.5

**Amount used:**
900 grams - 2183 metres/2387 yards

▷ *Hook*

4.5 mm

## How to make

Make 56 squares as shown in the table.

Join as shown in the schematic using the dc on back join from page 174.

Add the border from page 192.

| Pattern | Number to make |
|---|---|
| Look Behind Vivien (LBV) | 4 |
| Tall Taylor (Tall) | 4 |
| Billie Between (Between) | 5 |
| Invisible Jesse (Inv) | 5 |
| Turning Terry (Turn) | 5 |
| Same Same Sam (Same) | 4 |
| Popcorn Perry (Popcorn) | 5 |
| Other Round Ricky (Other) | 5 |
| Bob Leans On Flo (Bob) | 5 |
| Spiky Sid (Spike) | 5 |
| Merge Mel (Merge) | 4 |
| Coalesce Chris (Coalesce) | 5 |

| | | | | | | |
|---------|----------|----------|---------|----------|---------|----------|
| Between | Other | LBV | Between | Other | LBV | Between |
| Bob | Popcorn | Same | Bob | Popcorn | Same | Bob |
| Inv | Turn | Tall | Inv | Turn | Tall | Inv |
| Spike | Coalesce | Merge | Spike | Coalesce | Merge | Spike |
| Other | LBV | Between | Other | LBV | Between | Other |
| Popcorn | Same | Bob | Popcorn | Same | Bob | Popcorn |
| Turn | Tall | Inv | Turn | Tall | Inv | Turn |
| Coalesce | Merge | Spike | Coalesce | Merge | Spike | Coalesce |

# Glossary

## Abbreviations

| | | | |
|---|---|---|---|
| | cnr | corner | |
| | R | round | |
| | rep | repeat | |
| | **[RS]** | right side | |
| | sp/s | space/s | |
| · | ss | slip stitch | Insert hook into st or sp indicated, yo and pull through st or sp and loop on hook. |
| | st/s | stitch/es | |
| | stch | starting chain | Used in place of the first st in a round. Is included in stitch count. |
| s | stdg | standing | Attach yarn to your hook with a slip knot then work the stitch indicated as normal. |
| | **[WS]** | wrong side | |
| | yo | yarn over | Wrap yarn over hook from back to front. |

## Stitches — UK/US

| | | | |
|---|---|---|---|
| o | ch | chain | Yarn over, pull through loop on hook. |
| + | dc/sc | double crochet/ single crochet | Insert hook into st or sp indicated, yo, pull loop to front, yo, pull through both loops on hook. |
| T | htr/hdc | half treble crochet/ half double crochet | Wrap yarn around hook, insert hook into st or sp indicated, yo, pull loop to front (3 loops on hook), yo, pull through all 3 loops on hook. |
| T | tr/dc | treble crochet/ double crochet | Wrap yarn around hook, insert hook into st or sp indicated, yo, pull loop to front (3 loops on hook), 2x [yo, pull through 2 loops on hook]. |
| T | hdtr/htr | half double treble crochet/half triple crochet | Wrap yarn around hook twice, insert hook into st or sp indicated, yo, pull loop to front (4 loops on hook), yo, pull through 2 loops (3 loops on hook), yo, pull through all 3 loops on hook. |
| T | dtr/tr | double treble crochet/ triple crochet | Wrap yarn around hook twice, insert hook into st or sp indicated, yo, pull loop to front (4 loops on hook), 3x [yo, pull through 2 loops]. |
| T | ttr/dtr | triple treble crochet/ double triple crochet | Wrap yarn around hook three times, insert hook into st or sp indicated, yo, pull loop to front (5 loops on hook), 4x [yo, pull through 2 loops]. |

**Techniques**

| | | | |
|---|---|---|---|
| ⌢ | blo | back loop only | Insert hook into the back loop only of the st indicated. |
| | bp | back post | Insert hook around the post of the st indicated from the back. Can be applied to any st. |
| | cl | cluster | Numerous sts worked together as one st in the st or sp indicated. Begin the type of st indicated as many times as instructed. Work each st of the cl up to before the last yo and pull through 2 loops on hook, then yo and pull though all loops on hook. Could be any number of any kind of st. e.g. 4trcl, 5dtrcl, 3htrcl and worked as fp or bp. |
| ⌣ | flo | front loop only | Insert hook into the front loop only of the st indicated. |
| | fp | front post | Insert hook around the post of the st indicated from the front. Can be applied to any st. |
| | inv join | invisible join | Cut yarn after completing last st of round. Pull tail up through the last st, thread tail onto needle, insert needle under "v" of first true st of the round and back through the centre of the last st, and through the lbv of the last st. Pull tight enough to form a "v" on top of the stch, weave end away. |
| | lbv | loop behind v | The third loop or back bump of a st on the back. It's located under the back loop of a st. Any st can be worked into lbv, including cl and tog sts. |
| | mc | magic circle | Method used to begin a square. Wrap yarn around a few fingers, forming a loop, insert your hook into the centre and pull the working yarn through, ch1 to secure. Work R1 sts into the ring, pull the tail to close the ring once all sts have been made and secure by weaving the end in well. |
| | pc | popcorn | 5 treble crochet sts worked in the same st or sp, gathered together once all sts are made by removing hook, inserting it into the first st of the group and joining it to the last st of the group with a ss. |
| | tog | together | Numerous sts worked together as one st over a number of sts or sps as indicated. Work the specified number of sts up to before the last yo and pull through 2 loops on hook, then yo and pull though all loops on hook. "tog" will be followed by "over next # sts". It can be done with different numbers and types of sts. e.g. tr5tog over next 5 sts, dc2tog over next 2 sts. Can be worked as fp or bp. |
| | | at the same time | Shows where to place your hook when gathering sts from a previous round into one. |
| | spike | spike st | Insert hook into st or sp indicated, usually in a round more than 1 round prior to the current round, pull up a long loop level with the current round and work st as normal. Can be any st e.g. spike dc, spike tr. |

# Thank You

Wow! My eighth book! It would not have happened without the help and assistance of many folks. Many of these folks have been with me since the first book adventure of Granny Square Flair. I am so pleased to have them on my team.

Thanks, Michelle Lorimer, for your graphic design skills, bringing all my ideas into one cohesive book. I'd truly be lost without you.

Thank you, SiewBee Pond, once again for your wondrous technical editing and proofreading. Thanks to Amy Gunderson, for creating all the charts.

My pattern testing team were a boon to me as usual, testing all the patterns and charts. Thank you, Anne, Chantelle, Hayley, Jassy, Jennifer, Jenny, Judy, Kathy, Keri-An, Lyn, Marion, Meghan, Paulina, Rita, Ruth, Sam, Sharon, Shona, Tammy, Teresa, Terrii, and Ursula.

Thank you, Gretchen and Selena, for being the first to trial GSA2. Your feedback was invaluable.

Thank you to Bendigo Woollen Mills for supplying the yarn for me to make everything.

And lastly, thank you for choosing to continue you granny square adventures with my book. I hope it teaches you a lot and builds your crochet confidence.

xx Shelley

## About the Author

Shelley Husband is a prolific crochet pattern designer, publishing 10 books bursting with modern takes on the traditional granny square. Her first book, Granny Square Flair, won the best crochet book of 2019 in the UK.

Shelley has a real passion for designing seamless crochet patterns with the aim of teaching others through encouragingly supported patterns to create timeless, classic crochet heirlooms.

Based on Gunditjmara country also known as Narrawong in South West Victoria, Australia, when not designing and publishing new patterns, Shelley teaches crochet in person around Australia, and throughout the world via her online presence.

You can find Shelley online at her website shelleyhusbandcrochet.com.

# More Books by Shelley Husband

### Granny Square Academy

Learn all there is to know about making granny squares, including how to read patterns.

### Beneath the Surface

A beginner friendly pattern, with lots of extra support including video links.

### Granny Square Flair

50 written and charted granny square patterns and 11 project ideas to make with them.

### Granny Square Patchwork

40 written and charted granny squares patterns of 6 sizes and 12 projects to make with them.

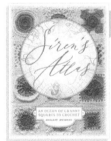

### Siren's Atlas

64 written and charted granny square patterns for adventurous crocheters.

### Nimue Crochet Blanket

A crochet quest of epic proportions with very detailed help including video links.

### Dotty Spotty

Classic circle-to-square granny square fun.

### The Cove

A pick your path pattern inspired by coastal adventures.

### Corners and Curves

45 Granny Square patterns for crocheters ready to play with colours, corners and curves.

**Buy my books direct from me in my shop or online at most online book retailers around the world. Visit my pattern shop for digital patterns galore.**

shop.shelleyhusbandcrochet.com

Made in the USA
Monee, IL
08 November 2024

69614915R00111